CU00970814

The 101 Principles of an Effective Leadership for Africa

The Sub-Saharan Realism

by Allen A. Alube

DORRANCE
PUBLISHING CO
EST. 1920
PITTSBURGH, PENNSYLVANIA 15238

The contents of this work, including, but not limited to, the accuracy of events, people, and places depicted; opinions expressed; permission to use previously published materials included; and any advice given or actions advocated are solely the responsibility of the author, who assumes all liability for said work and indemnifies the publisher against any claims stemming from publication of the work.

All Rights Reserved
Copyright © 2023 by Allen A. Alube

No part of this book may be reproduced or transmitted, downloaded, distributed, reverse engineered, or stored in or introduced into any information storage and retrieval system, in any form or by any means, including photocopying and recording, whether electronic or mechanical, now known or hereinafter invented without permission in writing from the publisher.

Dorrance Publishing Co
585 Alpha Drive
Suite 103
Pittsburgh, PA 15238
Visit our website at *www.dorrancebookstore.com*

ISBN: 979-8-88925-212-2
eISBN: 979-8-88925-712-7

The **101 Principles** of an **Effective Leadership** for **Africa**

The Sub-Saharan Realism

TABLE OF CONTENTS

ACKNOWLEDGEMENT

It is my pleasure to dedicate this book to my late and beloved father and mother Daniel and Lea Alube who inspired me throughout their exemplary lives over the years. Also, to my brothers and sisters Leonard, Justine, Therese, and Roger; and to my dear children David, Matondo, and Bianka for their outstanding love.

I thank all the friends at Miami Christian School, especially Judith Isaza for reviewing the manuscript in record time. I am grateful to Dr. Yeno Matuka of Ball State University in Indiana for his input and significant guidance; to Dr. Robert Mupier of Texas Southern University, Dr. Benande Makele of Arizona State, Dr. Victoria Steinberg of University of Tennessee in Chattanooga, Dr. Trevor Turner of Clark University in Atlanta, Georgia, Dr. Kawalie Fataki, Mr. Freddie Nsapo... for their solemn encouragement and support. And finally, many thanks to Susan Caylor from the English Department at Bradley Central in Cleveland, TN.

INTRODUCTION

The purpose of this manual is not to supernaturally or automatically solve the impasse of leadership in Africa, but to warn the African scholars and the civil society about their inaction regarding the collapse of African livelihood. Over the years, Africa has undergone difficult and tough times, and the trend is likely to continue unless radical actions are taken very soon to change the political moral values. African people must speak out and do something against poor leadership.

It may be time to remember the era and the generation of the African novelists and writers who once eagerly dismissed the mischievous behavior of a certain, alienated African elite, who blindly embraced the Western lifestyle in the '60s. By choosing to live a Western lifestyle in the African context, this group of people had traded values and responsibilities with corruption and mismanagement. They were unable to bring the change that the African people expected.

From Nigeria to Kenya, and from South Africa to Ghana, outstanding writers of the '60s such as James Ngugi, Chinua Achebe, Armah Ayikwe and Wole Soyinka truly influenced African literature in a most positive way. In most of Africa at that time, values and personality meant more than just material possessions and prosperity. The society was an inspiration, and its members tried hard to respect the established order. The chief spoke with clout, and therefore, his subordinates followed his leadership without restraint.

In most instances, the chief assembled his council and decided in consensus for the benefit of the community. It was believed that he was empowered with colossal wisdom and worked towards reaching specific goals.

By no means was the chief's authority seen as tyranny. The entire village cared for the welfare of its people, and anyone in the community could interfere in one's business provided no conflict arose. Meanwhile, stubbornness was quickly reprimanded; theft was severely punished; and prostitution was not only discouraged, but also scornfully mocked. However, the wave of rituals that once swayed Africans to cultivate the very traditions which made them unique is vanishing today.

Old traditions are now giving way to the international culture. Besides the globalization of economy and trade, the world longs to standardize belief systems, values, and everything else. The digital culture is affecting even remote villages in Mozambique, Guinea, and Cameroon. Rock-n-roll music, mobile telephones, and the worldwide web are just some technological innovations that are affecting or dictating our society today. Progress and highly developed technology is no longer the concern of the rich nations alone.

Unlike Manu Dibango or Tabu Ley Rochereau, young African music stars struggled to develop a sense of belonging to a trend; they vacillate between Western or American Hip Hop and their African Rumba, Soukous, or Makossa styles of music.

Politicians and other leaders can no longer trust their own institutions; often, they make appeal to former colonists, and they look at them as models and roadmaps for almost everything. The list goes on and on. French colonies like Ivory Coast, Gabon, and Senegal, for instance rely more on French advice while the British colonies like Uganda, Sierra Leone, and Kenya traditionally make appeal to Great Britain for all kinds of interventions.

Chapter One

AFRICA AND ITS DILEMMA

Like any other continent on the face of the earth, Africa was born with its share of natural and manufactured problems. It never was a perfect society despite the many positive aspects mentioned earlier. Nevertheless, more than 50 years have passed since most of Africa was granted its so-called freedom, also known as *Independence*. This mainly occurred in the '60s. Since then, quite a few generations have come and gone, and they all have faced different realities. One cannot address Africa's issues without having an overview of Africa itself.

First of all, it is important to remind our readers that Africa is not a country as many people outside Africa would like to think; it is a continent like Europe, Asia, or North America. In fact, according to the World Atlas: Millennium edition of 1999[1], the width of Africa is second only to Asia, and it covers an area of 11,712,434 square miles; that is 30,335,000 sq. km—including Madagascar. Therefore, those who minimize Africa's dimensions by considering it a country, often act out of ignorance. A few years ago, a gentleman from the state of

---

[1] Andrew Heritage, World Atlas: Millenium Edition (New York: DK Publishing Book, 1999), 120.

Tennessee asked me where I was from; when I replied that I was from the Congo, formerly Zaire, he became exasperated and asked: "Why can't you just say you're from Africa, man?'" According to him, Africa was just another country like the United States or Guatemala. Occasionally, out of ignorance, someone will ask: "What's the capital of Africa?" And to other people, South Africa stands for the whole African continent.

As Victor C. Ferkiss puts it in his book, *Africa's Search for Identity*, to understand Africa, one must learn about Africa's history, and its physical area and human settings. He singles out the size of Africa as the most important fact about the continent. He says, "Its land area is three times that of the United States including Alaska."[2]

For the purpose of our discussion, we will mention scenarios which have been tackled by some three different generations that have lived through both good and bad times over the past few decades. The first generation could be labeled the *Inheritance* generation; the second, the *Outcast* generation, and the third is the *Victimized* generation. The Inheritance generation fought the independence battle and took power from the colonialists. In the meantime, its militants created additional problems by accumulating power and supremacy, wealth and pleasure while excluding the next generation of young Africans known as the *Outcast* generation. This Outcast generation tried hard to make ways into the government, public institutions, and other sectors. However, only very few people could succeed thanks to a system of clientèle; this is the one made up of a well-positioned uncle, cousin, or fiancé who worked somewhere in the administration.

---

[2] Victor C. Ferkiss, *Africa's Search for Identity* (NY: George Braziller, 1966), 14.

Africa Map from free blank outline map of Africa May 2nd, 2008

According to the African concept of family or relationship maintenance, one should take good care of his or her own entourage while he or she is in charge. When this was not possible or became unmanageable, many young professionals simply fled their countries for a better life abroad. As a result, many African professionals migrated overseas in pursuit of better living conditions and better income earnings. Once again, Africa lost some of its best work force in almost every domain. The brain drain is contributing to impoverishing the continent.

The Victimized generation saw itself at the bottom of the ladder with a growing rate of unemployment, a high cost of living, and a lack of quality education and sustainable healthcare. In short, there existed inability to properly function as humans. Consequently, there grew rapidly among the populations of Africa a tolerable system of bribery, corruption, theft, vandalism, and other forms of social unrest.

As the Outcast Generation marveled and hoped to take over, conflicts arose between generations. Of course, the Inheritance

3

generation saw power and public administration handed to them on a platter. Many among them had not been prepared to take over or never expected to assume serious responsibilities in the government or the private sector. Accountability was a totally foreign concept to them. Their lack of experience in public affairs led them to act irresponsibly. Thus, they would sometimes mishandle and swindle government funds at the expense of the taxpayers. In fact, many of them had never had any experience even in private industry. That is why they did only what they could as long as they kept the colonist out of the public affairs and trade. Then the Outcast Generation saw their dreams shattered while the Victimized Generation could only envision total despair.

Decade after decade, African episodes of bad politics are being repeated. Sons and daughters of this great continent find themselves trapped, wondering how they got into this mess in the first place. Some people have questioned the Almighty God; some have questioned the very stagnant mindset of our people, while others have simply chosen to place blame on various issues and circumstances. There seems to be a growing paradox of complaints and criticisms, yet very limited considerations to the daily struggle that cripples the entire continent of Africa. As a people of the same continent and the same heritage, we have deliberately chosen to ignore the real causes of our problems.

As often as we share concerns and African issues among African Diaspora, brothers and sisters of the African descent, and friends of Africa, we discover how much more complex and perhaps ambiguous the African dilemma is. Nonetheless, despite divergences among tribes, languages, and physiological traits, the African predicament remains in many ways the same. From Botswana to Madagascar and from Mali to Sao Tomé Principe, especially Sub-Saharan Africa has kept the mainstream behavior due to the same kinds of traditions that several ethnic groups share. Despite enormous diversities among African cultures, the traditional behavior is pretty much the same: we can list some of the impasses which have placed most African countries among the poorest nations in the world, namely: AIDS, malnutrition, child labor, rape, famine, and civil war.

Africa, as a whole, remains unmovable when it comes to tribal or regional conflicts and atrocities. For more than four decades, a history of conflicts, bribery, corruption, and mismanagement in Africa has thus revealed Africa's inability to govern itself. We can cite, for example: the Aouzou conflict between Libya and Chad over oil possession in the '80s; the Eritrea and Ethiopia warfare; the Bakassi Island fall-out between Cameroon and Nigeria; civil wars in Sierra-Leone, Angola, Mozambique, Congo Brazzaville, Ivory Coast, Sudan, Central African Republic, and the most devastating and widespread manslaughter and wars in the Great Lakes Region where genocide took place in Rwanda, and where the Democratic Republic of Congo faced unprecedented massacres, looting, and the illegal exportation of its natural and mineral resources by neighboring Rwanda, Uganda, Burundi, and their Western allies.

Of course, Africa's colonization by the Europeans had kept the Sub-Saharan Africa about the same for decades. It is characterized by an absence of fair bilateral trade agreements in many domains. This is remarkable in the existence of one-way commercial transactions; no real foreign policies towards Africa, instead much more has contributed to maintaining the status quo. There is no question whether the Western World is to be blamed for Africa's misery. The different systems employed by the colonialists still prove that their primary motive was to nullify the African brainpower, its economy, its socio-ethnic make-up, and its structural fabric as a whole.

In his *Meet the Congo and its Neighbors*, John Gunther contrasts different European systems practiced in different colonies of Africa. Gunther specifically mentions three countries with three different tragic policies. He writes: "The British want to set their Africans free eventually, whereas the French want to make them part of France." Furthermore, Gunther describes the Belgian system as the one in the middle. He states: "The Belgians think it is madness for the British to let Africans vote when they are[3] still economically weak, and worse than madness for the French to work out an elaborate political structure which permits Africans to have full French citizenship and to elect deputies to Paris."[4]

Another realm of African conflicts has come from within, sometimes caused by the African people themselves, but sometimes stirred up by outsiders, the enemies of the black continent. Internal conflicts like tribal break ups, land disputes, some political disagreements and violence among partisans of different political parties have been very common in places like Senegal, Liberia, Somalia, Rwanda, the Republic of Congo, the Democratic Republic of Congo, Central African Republic, Sierra Leone, Ivory Coast and so forth.

These wars and conflicts have not only caused perpetual disturbances to millions of Africans already living in extreme poverty and misery, but they have also brought a halt to progress and potential economic growth of the nations. The African continent that once was a provider of resources to the colonialists has hence reduced itself to becoming a bread recipient. Poverty and unparalleled misery have reached unimaginable proportions, and foreign media like Cable News Network (CNN), American Broadcast Corporation (ABC), British Broadcasting Corporation (BBC), or Radio France International (RFI) cannot wait to broadcast about refugee camps in Sudan, Liberia, Zambia, and Ethiopia; the genocide in Rwanda; and the spread of HIV/AIDS. Topics like these often characterize Africa according to the mainstream media.

At the beginning of this twenty first century, Africa, especially the Sub-Saharan Africa, must take a drastic turn towards a positive change and a long-term stability or else it will continue to collapse. There

---

[3] John Gunther, *Meet The Congo and Its Neighbors* (New York, Harper & Row), 1959, 31.
[4] Ibid,31.

must be an extreme makeover in the leadership position for the continent to experience a new direction, new dreams, a new hope, and a new economy. It is time for us, as citizens of Africa, to critically re-think, reevaluate, and revolutionize our fate. We must relearn to understand the real causes of our lack of success in many areas and admit some of our own weaknesses before we can undertake sweeping changes that will point to progress in the days ahead.

Certainly, many of the African conflicts have originated from elsewhere; one example is the drive for control by the superpower nations which continue to harm Africa's development and progress. But we must stand up to stop other forces from driving and leading us. We must unite and combine our effort. Together, we can win this battle. In fact, there is no other way but to work together as a people. We, as African people, should learn to live above whatever divides us so that together we can stand united against the world superpowers and economies.

Chapter Two

CONSCIOUSNESS AND RESPONSIBILITIES

The thought of writing this textbook first emerged in 1990 with what politicians could call *Political Awakening* in Africa. Afterwards, Idi Amin of Uganda, a cruel dictator of his kind also known as a gangster according to *Scotland on Sunday*, had been deposed and died in exile at King Faisal Hospital in Saudi Arabia in 2003. Jean Bedel Bokassa of Central African Republic, a true cannibal and vampire who enjoyed massacring his fellow countrymen, was deported from France, and imprisoned in his own country, the very country he once monopolized and destroyed. *The International News* reports that Bokassa died in Central African Republic on November 3, 1996. And finally, Mobutu Sese Seko of Zaire, the Father of so-called African *Authenticity*, and a tyrannical money monger who literally robbed his own country, weakened politically and physically, saw himself in exile in Morocco until his death on September 7, 1997 with very little to be remembered except as a notoriety.

The change, which took place in Eastern Europe, and the collapse of the Soviet Union and its allies in the '90s shook some of the African nations, which desperately needed something new. The Republic of Benin, one of the African countries in West Africa, led the black continent with the idea of restructuring the government and political institutions. In their book *"Not Yet Democracy": West Africa*

Slow Farewell to Authoritarianism, Boubacar N'Diaye, Abdoulaye Saine, and Mathurin Houngnikpo give credit to the students at the National University of Benin for stirring up a movement of protest, which later would lead to the birth of what was known as *The National Conference*. The first and most successful National Conference took place in Benin and then elsewhere in Africa.[5] Indeed, a student movement, which prompted the massive demonstrations and strikes leading to the National Conference in the past, could in the future become a starter for another major change in the African politics. Some politicians believe that the idea of National Conference originated in France. Many French speaking countries of the African continent saw the idea of National Conference as a true means of fairness in the art of governing, a way of instilling responsible leadership, and an opportunity to overcome dictatorship. Unfortunately, despite the overwhelming support for the concept of the national conference by many countries, the English-speaking countries of Africa like Nigeria, Kenya, or Tanzania thought the idea was another French form of imperialism to its former colonies; therefore, they did not warmly embrace this concept of the national conference. In a sense, this reasoning from the English-speaking countries could be understandable as those nations see France implicitly taking charge of its French speaking Africa every time there is a political unrest. Under French ruling came in place organizations such as *Communauté des Etats d'Afrique de l' Ouest (CEDAO)* and *Union Douanière des Etats d'Afrique Centrale (UDEAC)*, both regional economic task forces modeled in French speaking West and Central Africa; the *Colonie FranÇaise d'Afrique (CFA)* common currency, and *Air Afrique*, the united Franco-Africa airline that went bankrupt in 2000 are very telling about French resettlement in Africa. French presence and interventions in French speaking Africa could not be

5 Boubacar N'Diaye, Abdoulaye Saine, Mathurin Houngnikpo, "*Not Yet Democracy": West Africa Slow Farewell to Authoritarianism*, Carolina Academic Press, (Durham 2005), 156.

denied. Nevertheless, some of the Western nations besides France and notably the United States, welcomed the idea of the National Conference and even conditioned their economic aids and money lending to the establishment of democracy in Africa because they saw in National Conference a sense of liberation and a real preface of democracy coming to Africa. While the English-speaking Africa showed little enthusiasm in the National Conference undertaking, perhaps the French speaking Africa thought of it as a way of counter attacking Commonwealth, the long-term English-speaking economic organization established worldwide.

Prior to the establishment of the National Conference movement, many African countries lived under dictatorial regimes. There was no freedom of speech at all; and many regimes did not tolerate the idea of opposition parties. The few and brave individuals or groups of individuals who stubbornly spoke out against the tyrannical governments became victims of jail, exile, or simply brutal death. South Africa suffered apartheid and racial segregation for several years: during the '60s, '70s, and '80s, countries like Libya, the Democratic Republic of Congo, Uganda, and Central African Republic were notoriously known as champions of human rights abuse. Countries such as Angola, Chad, and Sudan were significantly torn into pieces by long-term rebellions and civil wars.

Governmental institutions, college campuses, religious organizations, and many other entities in many African nations became polluted with corrupted politicians wanting to secure their retirements by any means. They controlled the media and caused fear among the populations who could not express themselves freely. It was common to spot secret agents almost everywhere including university campuses, buses, and restaurants. In brief, terror ruled most of Africa. However, with this idea of the National Conference, many African people believed they had reached a new era of hope. Newer leaders like Nicephor Soglo of Benin or Bishop Ernest Kombo of Congo Brazzaville made the headlines at that time.

Sadly, the National Conference idealism turned out to be another false liberation. Yes, it slipped again, and people's hope faded quickly, especially when certain governments deemed unnecessary the idea of organizing a National Conference in their countries. Most of these governments feared vengeance from their populations, which have been suppressed for many years. In Zaire, for instance, Mobutu's regime resisted the thought of organizing the National Conference for a while, but finally gave in due to the pressure from a longtime suppressed population. Cameroon, Gabon, and many other countries simply rejected the thought of a National Conference. The political outcomes of the '90s proved to be insignificant apart from a few gleaming successes here and there.

Possibly, the most successful model of a turnover sprang out of Benin, an undersized West African nation with a population of less than 9 million people. As a matter of fact, Benin became one of the first African nations to freely elect a former head of state, Mathieu Kérékou, who initially opposed the concept of National Conference in his country.

Just like the surging of independence in the '60s, the National Conference disappointed many of the African nations indeed. The Democratic Republic of Congo held the most controversial record of the forum. Several resolutions simply failed to take place according to the spirit of the conference and the transition was unsuccessful because of a power struggle. If the African people did not learn a great deal in the '60s after the so-called liberation from the European colonists, they surely derailed in the '90s when the National Conference failed to meet their expectations.

There have been lots of arguments among African elites whether Africa's independence should have waited a little bit longer. Those who support this theory argue that Africans in general were not well suited in the '60s to take over the responsibility of the public administration from the colonists since they had not been prepared well enough to take over. While this view sounds logical, the opponents of this view think just the opposite. In fact, many believe that it was too late to liberate Africa. That is why pioneers like Kwame Nkrumah of Ghana, Patrice Emery Lumumba of the Democratic Republic of Congo, Sekou Touré of Guinea, Barthélemy Boganda of the Central African Republic, Julius Nyerere of Tanzania, Kenneth Kaunda of Zambia, Jomo Kenyatta of Kenya and many others fought forcibly to liberate Africa.

However, today the question of whether Africa should have been liberated in the '60s may be irrelevant because Africa's dilemma is not in the liberation of the physical territory, but rather in the mindset of its people. Liberia's earlier freedom from the United States could have well led Africa in its attempt to establish durable democracies. The African American Registry indicates that Liberia became independent on July 26, 1847. Unfortunately, Liberia failed to provide a democratic leadership role for the continent. On the other hand, countries like Angola and Namibia with late liberation from their colonists did not learn a great deal from their African counterparts, which acquired independence in the '60s. Power struggles and long-lasting rebellion in Angola could have prevented millions of deaths and ensured a remarkable progress in a country that is potentially rich in mineral and natural resources. Therefore, it is needless to argue that Africa's dilemma is not in the physical liberation of its territory but in the minds of its people. Africans must shift away from a stagnant state of mind to a progressive thinking capacity, which will cause a positive reaction in behavior.

Several politicians and people of good will, including so-called specialists of Africa, have long deplored the absence of democracy and freedom of opinions in Africa. Some experts do link Africa's lack of progress and development with the absence of democracy. However, the African reality may be broader than the scanty expertise from the so-called specialists' view.

While Africa's lack of democracy can be a hindrance to its development and progress, the real issue may sometime be lurking in people's ignorance. In many countries, Africa's rural population makes the bulk of the continent's global population. The indigenous populations in many countries have had very limited education; they can barely read or write. For decades, education has not been their main concern. Farmers and fishermen can care less about education if they can earn a living from their daily labor. The few indigenous folks who have some basic education had made little impact in their lives or none at all.

Unfortunately, the lack of basic education has affected not only millions of adults, but also millions of children. For instance, John Deke, a local businessman from Itere, D.R.C. tells his daughter not to bother with too much education because he expects her to get married once she reaches the age of fifteen so that she can depend on her husband. John's culture expects every husband to be the bread winner and the wife a total dependent on her husband. You see, a few years ago, a scholarly working woman presented a real threat to her culture. Many African cultures still believe in male supremacy over the female. Thus, to let a female climb the social ladder would diminish the male's self-made power and control. As a result, the culture made it difficult for females to have equal access to education, governmental institutions including the military, and many other sectors.

In the past, many girls had been forced to marry men they had never met because marriage at that time was not the fruit of love between the groom and the bride. In fact, several marriages were pre-arranged among family members regardless of the girl's opposition. Several couples became husband and wife without having exchanged any words before their wedding. The groom did not even have to be present at the wedding. This is because family members' assessments were enough, or perhaps because girls hoped to marry young men who made a decent living in cities or towns.

A fifteen-year-old girl from Timbuktu could marry a 40-year-old man in Bamako where living conditions are more promising. Because of the mindset that a skilled working female could well tell her husband what to do while she was a teacher or worked as a lawyer, a typical African white-collar man would not put up with that kind of emancipation challenge. Also, the fact that an African working woman who would go on a business trip out of town, leaving her husband and children behind for a couple of hours, would almost be insulting to her husband.

This is mainly because an African man was not prepared to accept such a deal, which according to him would destroy the traditions of manhood in his society. An African man is aware of his supremacy over his wife because when it comes to understanding males' superiority over females, he believes in a woman's total submission even if it has nothing to do with the Apostle Paul's teaching in the New Testament about wives' submission.

This is one of the scriptures that has been taken out of context by the African traditionalists. In the past, the African male culture had been very dominant; it had deliberately invented several rituals and myths that excluded females from touching certain plants, working certain jobs, playing certain sports, eating certain kinds of food or special meals, which were supposedly reserved for men only. Sadly, such a culture could well encourage the African woman to believe that she was just a subordinate being to her husband instead of a comate.

So, before one talks about democracy and freedom of opinions, it is imperative that one can read and write and to understand his rights and freely express his or her own opinions. We believe that a decent educational program, a proper and achievable training, should be put in place to help third world populations bridge the gap between poverty and average living, between the elite and the uneducated, between males and females, between adults and children.

Talking about Africa's dilemma, it may be fair to say that only a few Africans of goodwill have attempted to critically think for the future of the black continent. It is pretty sad to say that Africans lack

15

coordination in their effort to establish basic rules of life. So far, they excel in selfishness; they think less of others.

Leopold Sedar Senghor, former president of the Republic of Senegal, and Nelson Mandela of South Africa, both unselfishly set a wonderful example in sharing power without bloodshed. From being a prisoner to becoming the head of state of his controversial South Africa, from relinquishing power to becoming a conflict mediator, Mandela, the most outstanding African leader of all time taught it all. In fact, according to Miami Herald Tribune of August 2007, Nelson Mandela had been honored with a statue at the Parliament Square in London, England, by the London Mayor, Ken Livingstone.

Like Martin Luther King Jr., Mandela had truly symbolized a peaceful fight for freedom, inspiration, and God-given wisdom. This African hero, born in South Africa on July 18, 1918, was the cofounder of the African National Congress Youth League, a more radical branch of the African National Congress. As William Tolbert, the former president of Liberia put it, "...I cannot and will never subscribe to anything that infringes upon man's fundamental freedom and human rights sacredly granted him by our great and beneficent Creator".[6]

Despite the consensus about Africa's poor leadership, one will agree that these exceptional leaders of the past truly had the heart for their nations in particular and Africa as a whole. They had demonstrated the spirit of unselfishness. As the late Laurent Desire Kabila stated, "To live a pompous and selfish life among poor neighbors must horribly stink."

Kabila, one of the prototypes of a true leader, could have possibly been misunderstood by his peers. Like Lumumba, N'krumah, or Sankara, Kabila defied those who underestimate Africa's ability to rise. Just like many of his predecessors, Kabila had some vision about restoring dignity to Congo and to the entire Africa. He fought towards redefining a real identity of Africa. With the courage and

---

[6] *http://www.liberian-connection.com/tolbert/tol_speech2.htm, April 28, 2003.*

determination to face Mobutu's 30 years of dictatorship, with his refusal to settle for less, he understood the role his country was going to play in Central Africa.

As rich and strategic as the Democratic Republic of Congo appears to be in Central Africa, it could play the leadership role in the region just like Nigeria would in West Africa, and South Africa in the Southern part of Africa. These nations could have well led and coached every other nation in Africa as much as possible.

Dr. Steven Metz, a research professor at the US Army War College, thinks that the Democratic Republic of Congo, former Zaire, could either become the locomotive of development or the destabilizing agent in Africa. In his study entitled *Reform, Conflict, and Security in Zaire*, he writes: "Among Africa's giants, none is more crucial than Zaire. Even on a continent that has experienced more than its share of crises and conflicts, Zaire is particularly tragic." Africa in general, and particularly Ivory-Coast, South Africa, Congo-Kinshasa, Congo-Brazzaville, Angola, Chad, Gabon, Cameroon, and Nigeria, possess what it takes to subdue misery, illiteracy, and ignorance. With their diamonds, gold, cobalt, copper, oil, cocoa, coffee, timber, rubber and much more, a lot could be accomplished. Unfortunately, greed and egotism have seriously crippled African leaders. In the past, the African elite and other experts on African affairs have wondered whether Africa has the ability to lead.

African leadership must re-evaluate itself. There seems to be little sense of responsibility, commitment, accountability, and humility among those who hold key positions. Complaisance has long characterized African leadership; African leaders must wake up now or else Africa will continue to pay the price of foreign domination and exploitation. Sadly, when African bureaucrats come into power, they have the tendency to be served instead of serving; they want to be leaders and nothing less.

In many instances they think that their nations owe them a great deal of gratitude and respect even though they do not deserve the respect due them by the populations. Leadership is a gift and must not be taken for granted; it is one's God-given ability to lead efficiently. It has nothing to do with the best education or the amount of money that one possesses.

In fact, true leadership requires humility and sometimes modesty. It cannot hurt nor suppress the very people we lead. For instance, King David of the Old Testament, the great warrior of his kind, one of the greatest and most illustrious kings Israel has ever had, was the last choice among his seven brothers, yet he accomplished so much that his name has thus remained a legend in Israel and in the Christian world. David was chosen from the wildlife while he served his father as a shepherd. He was the last person to be thought of after all his brothers were disqualified. So, David's example of humility should inspire some of us today.

Chapter Three

THE CULTURE OF DEPENDENCY

In the history of mankind, people of all nations have fought wars; they have conquered other civilizations and designed great architectural buildings and monuments. In fact, Egypt, which has one of the greatest architectural designers and possibly the most memorable and unforgettable nation on the face of the earth, happens to be an African nation. To try to view Africa as a low level and weak continent is a mistake. Like any other continent, Africa has its strengths and weaknesses.

History reveals that Africa has always been at the center of humanity. From the Old Testament to the ruling of the great empires such as Roman and British empires, Africa has always been involved on multiple facets. When communism and capitalism unjustly shaped the black continent, Africa paid the huge price of being exploited, since neither communism nor capitalism profited Africa in any positive way. And when World War I and World War II broke out, Africa was naively pushed into the mud since those African combatants had no idea why they had to fight the wars that did not engage them directly.

Africa has always played a significant role, whether by direct or indirect participation, in world affairs. Although some scholars have unsuccessfully tried to link Africa's dilemma to its race or culture, we disagree very strongly to such an unfair judgment. Every nation and every continent have a story of failures and successes. As a matter fact, there is no nation and there are no people that ever went from success to success in a permanent way. Failure has often preceded success. To try to classify Africa and its people as permanent failure is simply missing the point.

Before its independence on July 4, 1776, the United States of America suffered major defeats and the civil war between the Northern and Southern states did surely slow down progress. The death toll was high, and the country lost some of its brilliant men in uniform.

Despite differences in cultures and subcultures, African people can do a lot better if left alone and given the opportunity to organize themselves. African people are not necessarily of inferior genes or low mental ability; sometimes they may simply lack the spirit of determination and commitment to achieve great things like any other people on the face of the earth. Neither democracies, nor empires, nor kingdoms will make great nations, but those people who are willing and determined to excel.

Ms. Holly Brown is one of the African American legends who was willing to transform the lives of some sixty-six black children from Oakland, California, by financially supporting their education. Ms. Brown's personal and moderate income could have prevented her from helping, had she not been willing and determined to make a difference in children's lives. In an interview with ABC on June 3, 2003, Ms. Brown declared the joy of reaping the fruits of sharing. She can be proud of a testimony out of the ordinary. Today, Ms. Brown's story can inspire millions around the world.

Rosa Parks, an Alabama black female who refused to bow to the white supremacy order; Martin Luther King Jr., one of the civil right pioneers and devotee of peaceful protest in America; and many others have proved that black men and women are as equal as any other race created by God.

Concerning equality, we, African people, must understand that from divine creation, God the Almighty has equipped all people through Adam and Eve with the same knowledge, the same wisdom, and every other skill necessary for the routine activities and the functioning of the body despite of what secular psychology would like to say. Because God is all justice, there is no reason why He would grant one people with special knowledge and not the other. In the beginning, in the book of Genesis, God declared clearly: "Let us create man in our own image." Theologians tell us that this assertion does not necessarily refer to the physiological aspect of a human being, but rather to the spiritual and emotional aspects. Therefore, we believe that all human beings and races are equal and should appreciate each other. They should also treat others with full respect and dignity.

In his book *The Meaning of Democracy*, Saul K. Padover presents John Locke, the English philosopher, as an advocate of human equality. Padover quotes Locke who believes that if exposed to the same education and other life opportunities, all races will excel or fail equally. Further, Padover writes: "In regard to 'men of low and mean education' and such others as are sunk in ignorance and drudgery, it was wrong to ascribe their inferior status to heredity."[7] Thus, African people can rest peacefully believing that they too are as equal as Europeans, Americans, or Asians.

We have no reason to believe that we are an inferior race compared to other races on the face of the earth. In Part Two: "Selected Quotations on the Concepts of Democracy, Equality and Liberty" of *The Meaning of Democracy*, Padover mentions several quotations from several thinkers and politicians of the ancient and modern world, among them Aristotle, the Greek philosopher, student of Plato, and tutor of Alexander the Great who lived between 384-322 BC.

In his *Politics*: "When a number of flute players are equal in their art, there is no reason why those of them who are better born should have better flutes given to them; for they will not play any better on the flute, and the superior instrument should be reserved for him who is the

---

[7] Saul K. Padover, *The Meaning of Democracy: An Appraisal of American Experience*. NY: Frederick A. Praeger Publishers, 1963, 45.

superior artist."[8] Francis Weyland in his book *The Elements of Moral Sciences* said: "All men are placed under circumstances of perfect equality.

Each separate individual is created with precisely the same right to use the advantages with which God has endowed him, as every other individual. This proposition seems to me in its nature so self-evident, as almost to preclude the possibility of argument."[9] Ronald Segal, an African born of Jewish parents, strongly disagrees that blacks are less than other races. In his book "The Black Diaspora," he challenges Muhammed Abu Abdulah Ibn Battuta, the most widely traveled of the Muslim writers in 1352, and other travelers to black Africa for not paying serious attention to black African works of art in stone and clay, bone and ivory, wood and metal, examples of which would eventually come to be recognized as among the greatest achievements of the creative spirit.[10]

While equality among human races is very significant and crucial, it is also necessary to acknowledge that without *liberty or freedom of expression*, equality is immaterial. Padover must be right when he repeats John Adams, the second president of the United States of America, who held office between 1797 and 1801, in these terms: "God Almighty has promulgated from heaven liberty, peace, and goodwill to man... Liberty must at all hazards be supported. We have a right to it, derived from our Maker."[11] (*Dissertation on the Canon and the Feudal Law of 1765*)

At the beginning of the 21st century, African people need to find inspiration in their kinsmen living abroad, especially those brothers and sisters of the Americas who have survived cruel and despicable treatments. Despite deplorable living conditions and all forms of humiliations, former slaves in America have thus far demonstrated that they could equally excel if given the same opportunities, tools, and means. In his book Black Inventors of America, McKinley Burt

[8] *Ibid*, 92.
[9] *Ibid*, 97.
[10] Ronald Segal, The Black Diaspora. (New York: Farrar, Straus and Giroux), 1995.
[11] Saul K. Padover, The Meaning of Democracy: An Appraisal of the American Experience (New York: Frederick A. Paerger, Publishers 1964), 98.

Jr. mentions several black inventors of the United States of America, who had brilliantly defied those of so-called superior races, yet less known by the Africans from the motherland. According to Burt, some of those inventors were Andrew J. Beard (railway coupling), Granville T. Woods (airbrake, electric railroad, etc.), Richard B. Spikes (semaphore, automatic gear shift), Jan Matzeliger (shoe last machine), Norman Rillieux (sugar refiner), Frederick M. Jones (truck and rail refrigeration, etc.), and Elijah M. McCoy (lubricating valves). In his preface, Burt writes: "The tremendous influence of the Black Inventor upon American Industry and Culture is a force which is still structuring our society."[12] To make his point clearer, Burk refers his readers to check him out at the Moorland Collection of Black Patents at Howard University in Washington, DC.

Below is a selective patent and invention index from "Black Invention of America." (See Appendix, pp. 141-148.)

Inventor	Invention	Date	Patent
Binga, M. W.	Street Sprinkling Apparatus	July 22, 1879	217,843
Burr, J. A.	Lawn Mower	May 9, 1899	624,749
Butler, R. A.	Train Alarm	June 15, 1897	584,540
Church, T. S.	Carpet Beating Machine	July 29, 1884	302, 237
Marshall, T. J.	Fire Extinguisher	May 26, 1872	125,063
Winn, Frank	Direct Acting Steam Engine	December 4, 1888	394,047
Woods, G. T.	Steam Boiler Furnace	June 3, 1884	299,894
Woods, G. T.	Telephone Transmitter	December 2, 1884	308,876

---

[12] McKinley Burt Jr. *Black Inventors of America*. Portland: National Book Company, 1989, 7.

Besides several talents and skills in the technical fields, African Americans in America have giftedly expressed themselves in the areas of arts, literature, education, exploration, filmmaking, media, army, music, sports and, of course, social activism and politics. In their book *Black Light: The African American Hero*, Paul Carter Harrison, Danny Glover, and Bill Duke publish several names of black achievers for their determination, discipline, and heroism: Maya Angelou, Langston Hughes, Bill Pinkney, Oprah Winfrey, Colin L. Powell, Stevie Wonder, Bill Cosby, Louis Farrakhan, Jesse Jackson, and many more. Barack Obama must be especially mentioned for his recent achievement as first black man ever to get the presidential nomination of a United States of America's major political party. But most of all for his election as the commander-in-chief of the most powerful nation in the world, the United States of America. Tiger Woods also deserves a special place for a legendary golf player, as does Michael Jordan for basketball.

John W. Ravage is another writer who has revealed the presence of black Americans in the western traveling adventure. Ravage mentions several brave men, among whom is Isaiah Dorman, known as a guide and a translator of the Indian dialects. In *Black Pioneers*, Ravage writes, "Serving as guides from the earliest days of discovery explorations and western travel, black men accompanied U.S. geological mapping surveys, expeditions to Yellowstone country, and others such as the Lewis and Clark expedition; they were a part of U.S. military maneuvers throughout the West."[13] Ravage then pursues, "What little is known about Dorman derives from a few short texts about Custer's 'Black White Man' who accompanied him on several military and personal forays. The text refers to Dorman's skill with plains Indian languages and his repeated hiring by the government to lead expeditions as a translator and guide."[14]

---

[13] John W. Ravage, *Black Pioneers: Images of the Black Experience on the North American Frontier*. (Salt Lake City: The University of Utah Press, 1997), 73.
[14] John W. Ravage, *Ibid*, 74.

"World," one of the leading Christian magazines, depicts George Washington Carver as a great scientist of his generation. As a professor at the Tuskegee Institute in Tuskegee, Alabama, Carver won a national recognition in 1921 for his several peanut butter inventions. In fact, in his article *Carver's Affirmations*, Marvin Olasky believes that Carver saw himself as God's instrument throughout his multiple discoveries.[15]

If today other people and races from other continents have excelled in their enterprises, there are reasons to believe that Africans can succeed as well. Where other people and nations have failed, Africans could surely succeed if they would learn from other people's mistakes. Certainly, the modern Africa could have also succeeded if it had learned the way to success from other continents. It is necessary to remind the readers that even the antique Africa made inventors in almost every aspect of life. From art to architecture, from weaving to pottery, from literature to the judicial system, from calendar to carving, Africa has always been there with its oral prose despite the lack of written records in most cases.

As we embrace the area of success and achievement, we must point out that experience has always shown one thing: success does not come easily. It is the result of hard labor and commitment to achieve an assigned task. Thousands of professional people will agree that it took years of practice for people like Mohammed Ali, Michael Jordan, Tiger Woods, Jackie Robinson, Sammy Sosa, Shaquille O'Neal, Akim Olodjuan, Mutombo Dikembe, the Williams sisters, and many others to achieve success. As we all can consent, success, no matter in what race it manifests itself, is always accompanied with challenges, discipline, and commitment. Without these elements, success becomes meaningless, and without a price, success ceases to be success. Some have acquired wealth treacherously by not following the proper channels and have counted their wealth as success. But our view of success does not

---

[15] Marvin Olasky, *Carver's Affirmations,* World, February 2003, 36.

necessarily equate with wealth or fame. Real success resides in the way one influences others, or his environment positively, regardless of how much wealth or fame success brings.

According to Ralph Waldo Emerson, success is "To laugh much; to win respect of intelligent people and the affections of children; to earn the approbation of honest critics and endure the betrayal of false friends; to appreciate beauty; to find the best in others; to give one's self; to leave the world a little better, whether by a healthy child, a garden patch, or a redeemed social condition; to have played and laughed with enthusiasm, and sung with exultation; to know even one life has breathed easier because you have lived—-this is to have succeeded."[16] Other anonymous figures have defined success as follows:

Anonymous 1

"The meaning of success gives me direction in how I want, and try, to live my life.

Anonymous 2

"Success is achievement of something you have wanted to achieve."

Anonymous 3

"Success is the realization of a worthy goal."

Anonymous 4

"Success is happiness. If you are happy then you are successful. An unhappy millionaire is a failure. A happy pauper is a success."

Anonymous 5

"Success is relative. The more successful you are, the more relatives you have."

---

[16] Ralph W. Emerson, www.chebucto.ns.ca/Philosophy/Sui-Generis/Emerson/Success.htm.

Anonymous 6

"Success is about outward and inward satisfaction; it is about freedom, dignity and the ability to share and to leave a sound legacy." *Anonymous 7*

"Success can be equated with the attainment of self-satisfaction and self-actualization." *Anonymous 8*

"Success is self-satisfaction."

Anonymous 9

"Success is peace of mind and sense of accomplishment."

Anonymous 10

"Success is when you affect people's life and when you can live forever, i.e., the memories of your good work makes you live forever."

Anonymous 11

"Success represents the failure of society to tolerate all levels of achievement."

Chapter Four

THE FAVORABLE AND DOWNBEAT LEADERSHIP

Several people of the black continent have set the tone and continue to do so politically, socially, economically, and spiritually. Nelson Mandela, the former prisoner, and president of South Africa, Koffi Anan, the former United Nations Secretary General, Desmond Tutu, the South African Anglican Bishop, and many other unheard of African achievers are just a few examples. Prophet Simon Kimbangu, the former Congolese Spiritual Father who received God's anointing at the age of 30, has become another icon in the continent. According to *Christian History*, another Christian magazine out of Colorado Springs, Colorado, there exist many untold stories about African prophets, preachers, and evangelists who have mightily converted their own continent in the past.

Unfortunately, such great men of God were brutally suppressed, tortured, killed, or simply ignored by the Europeans who colonized Africa, and their calling will never be fully known here on earth. Steve Rabey, a freelance writer from Colorado Springs, believes that prophet Kimbangu became the catalyst for Africa's largest independent church.[17] In A Soul of Fire, Elizabeth Isichei writes about

---

[17] Steve Robey, *The People's Prophet*, (Colorado Springs: Christian History & Biography 2003), 32.

William Wade Harris, a Liberian activist who left his local ministry to trail across Ivory Coast to evangelize. Isichei affirms that Harris baptized 100,000 converts in 18 months.

In his article *"Holy" Johnson and the Ethiopian Church*, Ted Olsen talks about reclaiming a lost legacy of African priesthood. He mentions Johnson's conversion in a most simplistic way. Another African inspiration is James Johnson. Moved by the Psalmist in Psalm 68:31, "Ethiopia shall soon stretch out her hands unto God", James Johnson, a native of Sierra Leone, West Africa, became a born-again believer with God's help. And Olsen writes, "Johnson became a deacon at the influential Pademba Road Church and in 1866 was ordained as a priest."[18] It is time now for more Africans to begin to plow and labor hard and well. We have the arguments and skills to become successful if we learn to add real discipline and commitment to our existing effort.

Before we end this chapter, it would be good to answer the same kind of question we asked at the beginning of the chapter. The question comes from one of the African leaders, his Excellency Yoweri K. Museveni, President of the Republic of Uganda. However, anyone who has been following the turn of events in the Great Lakes Region of Africa for the past decade will agree that Museveni is not different from his African contemporaries. More than one observer is amazed by the title of his book *What Is Africa's Problem?* While Museveni has been presented to the world as one of the lead presidents in Africa, his politics have not embraced all Ugandans. As Museveni defies bad leadership in his country, he has forgotten that he has caused more harm than his two predecessors in the Great Lakes Region where millions of people have increasingly been killed and thousands of women raped. Observers wonder, "How can the Ugandan president give his support when his army invades the neighboring Democratic Republic of Congo with the support of foreign countries?"

At first, both Yoweri Museveni and Paul Kagame denied having any involvement in Congo. It was only a few months later that both

---

[18] Ted Olsen, *Christian History*, Issue 79, Vol. XXII, # 3, 14.

leaders were exposed after their troops were proven guilty of killing, massacring, and stealing in Kisangani, the Congolese Oriental capital city. Indeed, the former Ugandan leaders such as Milton Obote, Idi Amin, and Tito Okello were bad, but Museveni and his government have brought more tension into the Central African region than his predecessors did. Moreover, Museveni thinks that the biggest problem Africa has embraced is the lack of ideological independence. Like many of his African peers, Museveni does not believe he has done anything wrong during his many years in power. Other executives are to be blamed for every wrongdoing. "What Is Africa's Problem?"

It is poor and irresponsible leadership, Mr. President; then, there is lack of humility and lack of courage to admit mistakes. While President Museveni suggests that ideological bankruptcy is Africa's main problem, he should carefully look at his[19] own policy at home and in the Great Lakes Region. Why are there still rebel groups against his regime? As far as we know, there are still rebel and militia groups in southern Sudan and Northern Congo, fighting the Kampala regime. The most aggressive one is the Lord's Resistance Army, which Christian Monitor Science calls "The Ugandan Mystic Rebel group."

Leaders like Mobutu Sese Seko, Yoweri Museveni, Paul Kagame, Laurent Désiré Kabila, and Joseph Kabila have been placed in power by Western nations in order to serve their best interest. The following statement just confirms our argument; Marina Ottaway, the author of *"Africa's New Leaders: Democracy or State Reconstruction?"* writes: "Paul Kagame of Rwanda and Laurent Kabila of the Democratic Republic of the Congo have often been included in the discussions of the new leaders."[20] For the past few years, Uganda had been presented to the world as one of the model democracies in Africa. Ottaway sees Museveni and his government as a good example. She thinks that

---

[19] Elizabeth Kanyogonya, What's Africa's Problem? University of Minnesota Press 2000, 10.
[20] Ottaway, Marina, Africa's New Leaders: Democracy or State Reconstruction? Carnegie Endowment, Washington 1999, 29-44.

Museveni has rebuilt his nation, strengthened power and the economy, and has created institutions of authority.[21]

Needless to say that even the evangelical church in America has fallen into the trap of politics. The church tends to believe all pronouncements of the Department of State. Only few congregations have taken time to research the whole truth about Africa's politics for themselves. On the contrary, churches, which rely on the United States Department's advisory, often cancel mission trips in many parts of Africa for alleged security reasons.

Imagine Jesus cancelling a trip to Golgotha or the apostle Paul backing off his missionary trip for fear of the unknown circumstances. There have been a few churches with a great deal of ministerial work in Uganda, not because Uganda is the only needy country in Africa, but because it has been placed in a strategic position to serve Western interests despite Museveni's claim against the West.

For a while, in Central Africa, Joseph Désiré Mobutu became known as the only brave leader to bring unity, peace, and stability in the region. Mobutu served his masters well until the time he no longer was needed; then they had to coach someone else. We know who helped Mobutu succeed in his military coup in 1965, and we know how much Mobutu contributed to destabilize the peace process in Angola, Rwanda, and other parts of the continent. Africans have an ideological bankruptcy because they allow their fate to be determined by other people. Most of the decisions about Africa's politics have been made in western capitals: Washington, Paris, London, Brussels, or elsewhere. One in power, our elected heads of state rush to Europe and to the United States either to explain to their controllers their political vision or to ask for help, which is often given under scrutinized conditions and instructions.

African leaders are told with whom to be friends and from whom to stay away. Lately, in September 2007, China shocked many nations by announcing a huge socioeconomic deal with the rich Democratic

---

[21] Ibid, 83.

Republic of Congo in the amount of some 9 billion US dollars according to Kongo Times published online on January 13, 2009. As soon as this deal was signed, several so-called Congo benefactors, including IMF and World Bank, became irritated. Their structural economic adjustment programs have never alleviated any African country in the sense of the Marshall plan, which was accorded to Europe after World War II. On the contrary, such programs have only brought hardship to the African people. They are not designed to help but to take advantage of weaker nations.

Besides Congo, China has broken many other deals with other African countries. However, China's involvement in Africa's economy should not be viewed as a definite answer to the African dilemma. Africans must rise to their feet and take charge of their destiny. A good policy against corruption is very much needed as Emmanuel Luzolo Bambi, one of Joseph Kabila's advisors claimed. According to *LaLibre Afrique* of June 22, 2018, Mr. Bambi revealed that the DRC lost about 15 billion US dollars per year due to corruption and bribery. This is a great moment to learn the big lesson. Enough mediocrity has been enough. Therefore, let us reverse the course.

Chapter Five

THE WALLS AND MYTHS OF ETHNICITY

Today, in the age of technological communication, we hear views and ostentatious opinions on news reports almost every day. Unfortunately, some of the opinions can mislead the public, which by in large trusts every bit of the news and analysis broadcast on national and foreign media. Some reports can simply be tainted and are massive fabrications in order to sell a story. It takes a charming title or a good advertisement to persuade the public to buy a newspaper, a magazine, or simply to convince viewers. Politicians and economists often find their backups from leading papers and magazines like *New York Times, Washington Post, Newsweek, The Economist, Le Monde, Jeune Afrique*, and many others. But every conscientious person knows that titles do not necessarily match the reality.

From time to time, several opinions try to explain the reasons why there are constant tribal wars and rebellions in Africa. Some people have attributed the origin of these wars and rebellions to ethnic conflicts. They tend to explain the difficulty of managing a multiplicity of ethnic groups in a continent that God has so blessed with diverse tribal groups, an unprecedented multiplicity, which is a unique reality to Africa. From Chad to Mauritania, or from Guinea to Malawi, Africa is full of diversities. For instance, Cameroon alone, a nation of only 883.000 sq. miles, counts about two hundred tribal groups, while Congo-Kinshasa with its vast 2,345,000 square miles counts over four hundred tribes. In part, one will agree with the difficulty of handling conflicts among so many people who do not share everything around them. Differences in the spoken languages, food, traditional belief systems, and power hierarchy sometimes can be a serious handicap to unity and harmony.

Are there walls of conflicts in the African continent that emerge from the different ethnic groups? There are indeed several differences among the people of Africa just like there are differences among European, Asian, and Hispanic populations. Africa alone has several thousand ethnic groups and tribes; therefore, conflicts can be expected, and they will always erupt as long as the world exists. Africa is known for a rich diversity, and this diversity comes from the socio-ethnic makeup of its population. Even small countries such as Togo, Benin, Gabon, Equatorial Guinea, Botswana, or Lesotho, with less than 10 million people each, can still count more than ten tribal groups. Within each one of these nations, there exist many differences among the tribes and ethnicities. These differences can range from eating habits to spoken languages, from costumes to arts, and much more. But we are grateful to say that such differences do not necessarily constitute walls and should not become pretexts or excuses for wars and rebellions that constantly arise among our nations.

Once upon a time, our elementary legends and tales explained why the Mandingo people invaded the Mankes, and why the Haussas fought the Fulanis. According to the tales, nomadic Africans traveled in almost every direction, and they fought whomever they met on their way just for daily food since they did not grow crops at that time. Other reasons for conflicts could erupt from land appropriation, or inappropriate conduct that would bring shame or malediction to the people. Theft, disobedience, adultery, and prostitution were some of the shameful behaviors that were punishable by the society in the past. Generally speaking, African people are very hospitable; they live a community life and share generously. In the past when African warriors settled and established empires and kingdoms, many cultures lived together; they fellowshipped with neighboring villages. One could not tolerate to see others starve while they lived plentifully. In many cultures, elders scolded strangers for declining an invitation to share a free meal, or snacks, chikwanga, or palm-wine. Turning down such an invitation is still considered rude and offensive in many parts of the continent even today. In June 1999, while I was visiting my hometown in Central Africa, one of my old buddies became offended when I tried to pay for the meal that he had ordered for me at lunchtime. As his guest, I was not supposed to pay for anything because he had happily agreed to host me. I should have known better, but I acted silly like someone foreign to the culture. It is important to understand that in the past, African tribes had more in common than they probably have today. Neighboring villages celebrated important events together; they went hunting and fishing together; they married among each other's families. In short, it took the village much less time to accomplish much more. Farming and building are just a few of the tasks men and women performed together. One person's happiness was everyone's happiness and one's grief was everyone's grief, as well. As little as Africa had in the past, its people lived happily and consequently, they were healthier. Despite speculations about Africans' life expectancy in the past, some ancestors did live longer than thought. Evidently, life expectancy has become a quandary because of extreme poverty.

In the '60s in Little Mutoy, Congo, Mr. Matsula was known to have been the oldest man around his community. He possibly surpassed the hundred-year cap of age even though his birth date was unknown to the younger generations. At his death, Matsula looked healthy, despite his craggy age. Sometimes, the guess-age approach could be misleading. Since there were no birth certificates during the pre-colonial era, Europeans could only guess one's age according to the physical appearance. Therefore, the life expectancy report is not always as accurate as it is often published. This assertion can be backed up by the United Nations 2004 *Demographic Yearbook* from their department of economic and social affairs. "Errors in the age data may be due to a variety of causes, including ignorance of the correct age…"[22]Before the arrival of the Europeans, Africa knew neither organized crimes nor conventional wars; there were no massive movements of refugees as we see them today. In fact, bombs and machine guns or rifles that can slay thousands of people at once did not exist. Therefore, it is very wrong to always associate conflicts in Africa with ethnicity only.

However, those who are aware of the Superpowers' foreign policies on Africa will testify that many of the wars and conflicts in Africa are the results of several attempts by those wealthiest economies of the world to continue to exploit Africa's resources. Many superpower nations have ways to impose their will on developing countries even though the tendency has been to deny any direct involvement in the internal affairs of the poor nations. Because of naivety, bribery, corruption, and lack of maturity and experience on the part of our leaders, the wealthiest economies often take advantage of African countries and their populations. Not only do they exploit, but they also monopolize and control the fragile economy that Africa tries to develop.

There is no need to line up statistics upon statistics to prove the above argument. Facts speak for themselves. One of the dreadful and hazardous tragedies occurred in Ivory Coast capital city in summer of 2006. On November 23, 2006, International Herald Tribune wrote an article about a lethal toxic slick, which was dumped in Abidjan on August 19, 2006; it had fatal consequences. In her article, Lydia Polgreen writes, "At least ten people died, and thousands were sickened after chemical waste pumped from a tanker chartered by a Netherlands based oil trading company was dumped across Abidjan, the economical capital of Ivory Coast, in the main landfill and near poor residential neighborhoods." Tragedies like

---

[22] United Nations, 2004 *Demographic Yearbook* 5th-6th Ed. (New York: 2007), 5.

this are recurrent in Africa because its governments are careless and sloppy in protecting lives effectively. Many African governments are to be blamed for accepting anything to accommodate European or American businesses and investments.

But African governments alone are not to be blamed. Many African consumers would rather shop imported goods and food versus the locally made ones. In fact, every concerned Nigerian, Kenyan, or Ugandan should know how much the British economy and lifestyle have shaped their countries. In the same manner, in Burkina Faso, Senegal, or Gabon, people take great pride in importing the French culture to the detriment of their own. From speaking like a Parisian to behaving like one, seems to be every young person's drive in the streets of Brazzaville, Douala, Abidjan, or Dakar. Sadly, many of our people have associated happiness with material possession, while happiness comes from within. However, not everyone in Africa believes the worldview which says that money and wealth alone make a happy living.

While studying abroad, many of us have come across thoughtless questions from classmates on college campuses or co-workers at the workplace. People often wonder whether in Africa we sleep in beds, eat bread, or put on shoes. The fact that Africans eat different, talk different, or dress different should not matter. Great people are known by their ability to love, to perform duties that benefit themselves, others, and the society they govern according to God's law, not by how much they possess.

Unfortunately, even some of the African descendants have misled their children and grandchildren into the egocentric and materialistic way of the modern world. In addition, many of the African immigrants have simply embraced the lifestyle that sometimes may be shocking: expensive mansions, cars, pompous lifestyle, and other careless expenditure. Very few African patriots living in the western hemisphere have strived to maintain a coherent, if not a balanced lifestyle while enjoying the excesses of their host countries.

Sylla Mohammed, a West African Ph.D. immigrant to the United States can be proud of his family for keeping up with his Sierra Leone basic traditions. Mohammed has worked in several southern states as an environmental engineer. In the summer of 2003, in a conversation with Dr. Mohammed, he related some of the boundaries he has established in his home that his family does observe while preserving their home-based traditions. After spending more than a decade in the U.S., Mohammed's entire family faithfully speaks Mandingo language at home, dresses up in the African attires of West Africa on important gatherings, and strives to eat together mostly their Sierra Leone's main food. He is one of the few African immigrants who have made a significant impact within his family. Items important to his culture such as African attire, food, music, newspapers, and much more are easily found around his home. Regrettably, many African immigrants believe in the westernization of their culture. This has less to do with adapting themselves to the reality of their host countries; some try by all means to intermingle themselves into a culture that is not theirs. Unfortunately, the same western culture that African immigrants embrace is slowly invading Africa, as we mentioned earlier.

African theatres project American and European movies weekly, including nude and pornographic materials. Disco, Rock and Roll, Hip-Pop lyrics and foreign music seem to be the way to go. Leather jackets or fur, which is commonly worn in wintertime elsewhere, can sometimes become a style in sub-Sahara Africa, where the temperature often averages 80 degrees Fahrenheit year-round. Homosexuality is finding its way and fast-food including Coca-Cola products are just a few to name importations.

Ali A. Mazrui, director at the Center for Afro-American and African Studies and professor of Political Sciences at the University of Michigan, talks about a clash of cultures. He sees the African elite struggling between their own culture and that of the west. Professor Mazrui writes, "Clearly Africa is not the nearest in culture to the western world, yet the continent has indeed been experiencing perhaps the fastest pace of westernization this century of anywhere in the non-western world."[23]

As much as Africa can appreciate western civilization and the age of industry and information, it must strive to keep its own identity just like Japan, Korea, or China have so far. In November 2002, while eating at a Japanese restaurant in downtown Chattanooga in the state of Tennessee and for the first time using Japanese chopsticks, I was amazed. I very much appreciated the oriental culture and identity that make them proud of themselves. Other experiences have come from my encounters with the Chinese culture, and with Indian and Latino friends, who keep up with their own cultures. Africa has yet to experience the progress the rest of the world has made thus far. Even though Africa is able to shine brightly in a few areas like African attires or crafts, African safari, biodiversity, there is much more to be done.

Sometimes one wonders why we African people seem so divided with so much facing the continent. The truth of the matter is that European colonization took away so much of Africa's heritage that it will take years of retraining the minds and behaviors. Whenever people's roots have been destroyed, it becomes difficult to rebuild on vacant ground. History teaches how new frontiers had been forged to meet the European agenda of division, exploitation, and easy control of the continent's wealth at the Berlin Conference of 1884 1885.[24] Tribes and families were cut off between two to three countries. Therefore, in many cases today, people of the same origin and ethnicity find themselves in two or three different countries, which they never chose. This is the case of Nigeria and Chad with the Hausa people, Ghana and Togo with the Ewe people, Angola and Congo with Zombo people, and Gabon and Cameroon with Beti people.

Probably the most devastating reason why Africa seems so divided is the power struggle and the structure of the economy. With the

---

[23] Ali A. Mazrui, *The African Condition* (New York: Cambridge University Press, 1980), 46-47.

[24] www.homestead.com/wysinger/berlin-conference-doc.html

introduction of the European political system, Africa embraced a system that was foreign to its hierarchy. Empires, kingdoms, and other forms of tribal institutions began to fade and almost became obsolete to the great satisfaction of the masters.

As strange as it may sound, all African kings and emperors were not ineludibly dictators in the way they have been portrayed today; they were instead rulers who imposed a certain discipline and took care of legal matters for their own communities and villages; they made sure that order was re-established whenever it was disturbed and believed that man's dignity was to be cautiously privileged. In *Early and Medieval African Kingdoms*, Ginger Norton mentions Early African Kingdoms Kush in Nubia, once ruled by Egypt, and Axum in Ethiopia. Then Medieval Kingdoms of the Sudan: Ghana, Mali, and Songhai.[25] As far as our memories go, there was no capital punishment in Senegal or Ivory Coast; there was neither hand nor ear chopping mechanism within the African society. According to the tales, there were, indeed isolated cannibal malpractice in certain localities under certain cruel kings who were not always popular. Nonetheless, in taking this position, our intentions are not to justify inappropriate behaviors of the ancient practices of the African people, but to establish the truth as much as we can and to help those who will be interested in learning a little bit more about Africa's fate, and hopefully inspire the African nations in a more positive way.

Broadly speaking, most of the African countries have given up their rights, their freedom, and their patriotism for few foreign trades, illegal deals, and ill-intentioned business contracts. As a resourceful continent, Africa has a lot to offer if the African people see the need to unify their strengths and work together on their weaknesses.

According to the African Development Report of 1997, several natural and mineral resources make up the bulk of African export. Among these resources are major food production, major non-food production, agriculture commodity, metal and non-metal mineral, oil

---

[25] Ginger Norton, *Early and Medieval African Kingdoms* 2004., Grade 4.

production, and much more. Such resources if managed properly could otherwise prosper Africa and the entire world.

David Fick, who writes about economic opportunities in Africa, details a variety of resources that the continent possesses. He believes that with countless resources, Africa's economy can be revived. However, Fick notes some of the biggest challenges facing the black continent: the fluctuation of currencies, corruption, wars and ethnic conflicts, lack of local capital, and lack of infrastructure. While these challenges are predictable and real, the need for a radical leadership cannot be overlooked. That is why we strongly advocate a drastic change in our leadership: a leadership of action, a leadership that will move Africa to the next level. Once a strong leadership is established, good planning and management will follow and then the economy will rise again.

As we may recall, in the '60s, Africa became a theatre of civil unrests and disturbances when the independence movement sprang up all over the continent. It took some of the western world by surprise since some of them never believed in Africa's most resolute revolution. It was unimaginable for the stronghold of colonization to learn Africa's argument about becoming a free and a sovereign continent. Many African pioneers of the colonial era then knew that they could organize themselves politically, economically, and socially. They understood that African people could decide for themselves about the future of their nations; they could sell their natural and mineral resources by influencing the prices of their commodities, and not expect to hear from someone else. They also knew that they could choose their trade partners as they wished. Even with outmoded economies, they knew they could feed their people decently. During that period, many of the African youngsters who are in active life today had not yet been born or were very little when the battle for Africa's independence broke out. Thus, they know very young about the complexity of the struggle of becoming free first spiritually, ethically, and economically.

For instance, Mr. Deo Kalala, now a district administrator, was born before 1960 when the socialist Mulele's uprising hit the heart of Bulwem area in the Bandundu province of Congo Kinshasa. Kalala still has a great deal to learn about why his country has been facing so many troubles. In Nigeria, Ghana, Congo, and in many other African nations, bribery and corruption in public administration have become a norm to obtain a faster service. "The Under the Table Deal" is common almost everywhere. Such a negative practice has been passed onto younger generations of the continent. In fact, in some places today, the refusal to either bribe or be bribed characterizes one as coward. Bribery and corruption rule from the chief executive officers to the middleman. In Congo for instance, the majority of college graduates averaging 30 years of age presently were born under Mobutu's regime of bribery and corruption. They have it all, from bribery to fraud, or from treachery to dishonesty. Imagine Mwana-May, born in 1977 just two years after Mobutu's coup that brought him to power; he went to school when the Congolese school system had been crippled by the corruption of the regime.

Sadly, Mwana-May's worldview is limited to Mobutu's philosophy of life: "Get all you can for yourself and your entourage." Beat down others if you can, provided you make your way out. Another counterproductive quote is that "It is all right to take just a little bit if there is a need," said Mobutu. But in reality "take" in this particular context is simply a metaphor for stealing. In other words, bend the rule just a little bit, steal just a little bit from wherever you work. In short, Mobutu's doctrine consisted of the end justifying the means. Today, all Mwana-May knows and appreciates is the experience of a valueless lifestyle he has received under a spineless regime, which cared less about morality, honesty, and doing the right thing.

In the spiritual realm, things had not been easier either. Simon Kimbangu, a prophet from the Kongo ethnic group in western Congo, was denied the right to proclaim the gospel of Jesus Christ to his fellow Congolese because of his race. According to the Belgian colonial priesthood and government, there was no way God could reveal Himself to an African slave through a divine vision. Kimbangu, then, found himself in jail for preaching the word. While in jail, he endured all kinds of abuses and molestations before his assassination. As of today, without the Europeans' assistance, Kimbangu's ministry has grown beyond Congo. Despite such a growth and worldwide recognition, western missionaries continue to minimize the impact of *Kimbanguism*. In fact, some of them consider it to be a cult.

Politically speaking, lots of things could have been accomplished by the pioneers if there was no intrusion in the internal affairs of the black continent by the world superpowers and giants. There is no doubt in the mind of the African people that Europe and America had always had joint efforts to impose their will on African countries. Those who deny such a reality must re-learn history if they want to be honest with themselves. In their *African Crisis Areas and U.S. Foreign Policy*, Gerald J. Bender, James S. Coleman, and Richard L. Sklar compiled several writers who had critically written about African crises, namely those that occurred in South Africa, in the Horn of Africa, in Zaire now the Democratic Republic of Congo, and other countries. The editors openly condemn America's foreign policy towards these African nations and regions. They particularly blame the United States and the former Soviet Union for internationalizing Africa's conflicts. They see this course of action in three possible areas where they see both superpower nations adding up to the internal and already existing discords. They write:

"Although there is powerful internal dynamics of escalation inherent in the interactions of adversaries in any crisis, the escalation of a local crisis to the level of cold war engulfment is significantly furthered by at least three generic pushand-pull forces and influences in the external environment of the crisis: (1) the overall structure and ethos of the prevailing international system; (2) the perceptions and motivational assumptions of the two super powers regarding each other in their global competition for parity, which psychologically each interprets to be primacy; and (3) the penetrability of the African crisis by external powers."[26]

At graduate school, one of my South-Asian schoolmates from Burma agreed with me when we both shared our overseas life experience as to how our distinct communities think and behave. We both exchanged thoughts about how African and Asian people would generally settle their differences. As ludicrous as it may sound, in both of our cultures, we talked about how many people who often engage in verbal disputes will sometimes end their disagreements in a physical clash then comes peace at the end of the fight when both parties are exhausted. On rare occasions, do people resolve personal conflicts in shooting, except for some isolated cases, which no one tolerates anyway. Fighting is a practice widely spread in many parts of the world. So, in essence there is really nothing like *"killing someone with a smile."* African people do express their annoyances openly. This brings us back to how external forces play a key role in most of Africa's conflicts. Some of our closest friends and allies do not hesitate to stir up conflicts, rebellions, and border divisions so that they can have a better control of the situation.

In his study, *South African Policy and United States Options in Southern Africa*, Sam C. Nolutshungu believes the West to have strongly been the pro-minority apartheid regime of the former South Africa for several decades. He stipulates, "On the question of South Africa, Western policy, for nearly four decades, has been dominated by two beliefs: that the white minority regime is not only staunchly pro-West, but that it is, in a deeper economic and racial sense, and growing economic and military interests to be maintained and advanced in South Africa, which the West collectively cannot renounce without some inconvenience to itself."[27]

---

[26] Gerald J. Bender, James S. Coleman, and Richard L. Sklar, *The African Crisis Areas and U.S. Foreign Policy* (Berkley: University of California Press, 1985), 7.

[27] Gerald J. Bender, James S. Coleman, and Richard L. Sklar, *The African Crisis Areas and U.S. Foreign Policy* (Berkley: University of California Press, 1985), 49.

Obviously, interference in Africa's internal affairs does not help Africa nor does it help the Western world in a real sense. It can only help the few, the super and prosperous class of the rich people. No one deserves to be exploited recurrently in the new millennium. In the pre-colonial years, it was evident that the average European did not directly become wealthier from Africa's resources. Probably, the best example is seen in Central Europe where the average Belgian citizen might have not benefited straightforwardly from Congo's resources that King Leopold II monopolized. For 80 years, history tells us that Congo as a nation was the private property of King Leopold II of Belgium, and that every resource that was exploited and carried away from Congo belonged to the royalty. History will judge those superpowers and their allies who continue to exploit and impoverish Africa today. Some have claimed that they only try to help poor nations of Africa, but the reality is that those governments who give to Africa expect hundred-fold in return one way or the other. For decades, most help to Africa had been in the form of machine guns, bomb and explosive supplies-arranged military coups, assassinations, etc.

In *African Crisis Areas and U.S. Foreign Policy*, Crawford Young writes about "The Zairian Crisis and American Foreign Policy." In this chapter, Young criticizes American intentional plans to make Congo a display model for its aid program to the Sub-Saharan Africa. He mentions how the West evidently rushed Congo Leopoldville into an unprepared independence. With only a handful of trained Congolese, the Belgians and their friends knew that Congo would be on the blink of civil war, chaos, and anarchy when they calculatedly flashed the 3rd largest African nation into a masquerade which they called "independence." Young states, "The sudden and unexpected surge to independence in 1960 triggered improvised American plans to make the Congo a showcase for its newly launched African aid program. When 'crisis' and 'chaos' intervened, the United States became the principal force underpinning the U.N. operation, and the primary external patron of the struggling Kinshasa regime. The 1965

47

Mobutu's coup, which swept away the first Republic, occurred with American blessing (to put the matter modestly)."[2829]

Professor Nzongola Ntalaja, one of the Congolese figure writers, makes an intense breakdown on the U.S.–Zaire relationship. In his *"United States Policy toward Zaire"* commentary, he discusses the nature of the relation. He mentions U.S. involvement in Zaire politics before and after Congo's independence in 1960. Ntalaja describes this involvement as a failure because of its negative consequences on Zaire and the entire continent of Africa. He sees Congo becoming the victim of a conflict between the superpowers of the eastern and the western worlds. Ntalaja writes, "U.S. and Western involvement in Zairian affairs has not only undermined the process of institution building, it has also had the effect of prolonging the crisis of the Zairian state and society."[30] As strategic as Congo was in Central Africa during the era of the Cold War, both the United States of America and the Union of Socialist Soviet Republic used their might and money to sway Congolese authorities, each pulling Congo on their side. The Democratic Republic of Congo, surrounded by nine neighboring countries, had its own shares of problems to deal with; then its neighbors' saga almost every day. Congo did not need additional conflicts it could not handle. The zeal to win Congo by both superpowers resulted in bloodshed, several rebellions, the destruction of infrastructure, the holding back of the frail economy, and desperation and anarchy among politicians.

By this time the United States, through the Belgian government, had encouraged the political or physical elimination of some key Congolese figures and politicians like Patrice E. Lumumba, Joseph Kasa-Vubu, and a few others for their patriotic views that were misinterpreted by the West. For instance, Lumumba was accused of having had ties with the communists and would shortly be assassinated

---

[28] Gerald J. Bender, James S. Coleman, and Richard L. Sklar,
[29] *Ibid.*
[30] *Ibid,* 217.

in January 1961, only one year after Congo's independence. In Congo, Lumumba is considered to be the father of Congo's independence and has been elevated to the rank of a *National Hero*. Lumumba is also well known in Africa and around the world for his non-violent fight for freedom for his country. On the other hand, the Soviet Union had launched rebellions from several fronts in Congo in the '60s. Ill-trained rebels came into war committing all kinds of atrocities among peaceful civilians. Killing, looting, raping, and every imaginable abuse became a common practice.

In 1960, when Congo became independent, I was only three years old, but some two years later, I heard the triumphant singing of June 30, 1960 during the celebration of Congo's independence that supposedly meant freedom at last, sovereignty, victory, fairness, and prosperity. The popular song and slogan "Independence Tsha Tsha... O Lumumba Tsha Tsha... O Kimpwanza Tsha Tsha, to gagner..." were some of the slogans and tunes that brought hope to millions of the Congolese people. Regrettably, the celebration only lasted for a short period of time. With the confusions at the top level of the Congolese political leadership, and with the despicable murder of Lumumba and several other nationalist figures, Congo was breaking apart.

Several provinces such as Katanga, both Kasai provinces, and the North-Eastern region were in turmoil. Some of these provinces had declared their autonomy with self-imposed transitional governments. Many provinces of the nation became disconnected. In the meantime, an uprising that erupted in 1963 reached the district of Kwilu in my Bandundu province.

For the first time in my life, I saw rebels at work. They looted systematically and destroyed everything on their way. They beat and abused innocent people, raped nuns, and committed other atrocities daily. Schools were shut down for about four years, and the local administration ceased to operate. There was no health care system available because all local clinics no longer received medical supplies.

The Kwilu ordeal, also known as Mulele rebellion, forced peaceful civilians to flee and to spend between three to five years in the jungle and bivouacs. As a child, I cried and wondered why we had to experience such adversity.

With the help of the West, Joseph Desire Mobutu succeeded his military coup in November 1965. With a challenging mission to end the rebellion, he dispatched several troops of the Congolese National Army around the troubled areas. These men were supposedly sent to re-establish order and bring peace, but sadly, they too tortured, raped, killed, and caused fear among the local people. I saw unimaginable scenes, and I became seriously traumatized. Josphine, uncle Luka's wife, could no longer bear the struggle of having to care for her 6-month-old baby who cried day and night. With the fear of being spotted by the armed forces of the government from Kinshasa, she then decided to bury alive her own baby boy. Uncle Daniel Bula-Bula, my cousin Edison Pasula, and Pierre Ndulu of the Elanga village were killed about the same time because of their loyalty to Pierre Mulele, the socialist head of the Kwilu rebellion. I also saw Uncle Paul Nio-Nio, Joseph Mulenga, and other people of the surrounding areas with chopped off hands and ears for supposedly not complying with the military orders. It was not only horrifying, but also and naturally inhumane. My own father and several other people would be murdered a few years later. Tortures and several massacres continued at the same time in the Bulwem area near the city of Idiofa. Perhaps Idiofa was the most hit area of the district. There was no one single journalist, reporter, or independent agent associated with human rights in the area. Most of the killings and atrocities have thus far remained untold or unrevealed.

My father's murder has been the most devastating life experience for my family and myself. Even after so many years, the brutal assassination still brings back the bad memories that my family will never forget, and the story deserves to be heard. Today, there are many more untold stories of massacres across Africa.

In the Eastern part of Congo Kinshasa and elsewhere in Africa, many more people are being brutalized, beaten, threatened, and even killed daily. Like my family, thousands of families suffer from anxiety and hopelessness because they have not been able to recover from the loss of their loved ones. Often, murder cases perpetrated by African governments remain a mystery. No one dares investigate for fear of reprisal. Since most African governments control the judicial system, the average family finds it useless and fruitless to fight their corrupted governments anyway.

In *The Impact of War on Children*, Graca Machel, a well-known international advocate for children and a founder and president of Fundacao para o Desenvolvimento da Communidade, a community foundation in Mozambique, writes extensively on the negative effects of war on children worldwide. She raises concerns about child soldier scheme, children's health, sexual violence, and exploitation of children and so forth... As a way of preventing wars and resolving conflicts, Machel suggests that the international community crack down on any political environment that may cause conflicts. She recommends: "The best way to protect children from wars is to prevent conflict. The international community must shatter the political inertia that allows circumstances to escalate into armed conflict and destroy children's lives."[31]

In Eastern Congo, Liberia, Sudan, Somalia, Sierra-Leone, and other parts of Africa, child soldier patterns became prominent for a while. The war advocates often massively recruit children and move them up to the front line where they shoot anyone in their way including women, older folks, and their age mates.

While we appreciate Mrs. Machel's appeal to the international community to help prevent conflict in Africa, we still believe that our local governments in Africa have a mandate to secure their given territories by providing the suitable political atmosphere to their populations. The international community can only do so much for

---

[31] Graca Machel, *The Impact of War on Children*. New York: Palgrave, 2001, 182.

the entire humanity. That is why Africa should not always expect every bit of solution from the international community. It must take things into its own hands before counting on the outside world.

In 1994, the Rwandan genocide could have been prevented had both rivals Hutus and Tutsis looked beyond their tribal differences and agreed to live together as one nation. In South Africa, the African National Congress (ANC) and the Inkatha Freedom Party (IFP) militants could have well formed a coalition to fight apartheid had they resolved to collaborate.

In fact, much more could be said about collaboration, togetherness, and unity.

Chapter Six

RE-TRAINING THE AFRICAN LEADERSHIP

Besides the need for a strong leadership in Africa, there is another area where help is most needed in Sub-Saharan Africa: literacy, health care, freedom of speech, human rights, gender equality, or the fight against social injustice and corruption. Nonetheless, literacy in my view would be the key ingredient to resolving many issues in the African society today. The need for literacy cannot be over-emphasized. More than anything else, African people must win the fight against the syndrome of illiteracy that causes many people to remain ignorant and fragile. Ignorance is a disease that can be eradicated if our governments see it as a priority and are willing to take acute and radical actions. Ignorance can no longer be tolerated among our people. It is a huge mistake to continue to think that ignorance will go away by itself. African professionals and officials must act now. Our people can still be educated and be taught well if they are given the opportunity and necessary tools. It is never too late to learn because people do learn every day anyway. As Derek Bok said in *Business Week Online* of July 10, 2006, "If you think education is expensive, try ignorance." Our governments must do whatever it takes to educate African people through adult literacy, workshops, seminars, or any other forms of continuing education.

Having been part of the Adult Literacy program in the state of Tennessee, I have seen people like John, a 70-year-old male and a retired truck driver come back to school expressing the earnest desire to learn how to read and write. Cathy, another inspiring 55-year-old female had come back to school to prepare for her General Equivalency Diploma (GED), which is the equivalent to the French high school Baccalauréat. Cathy's goal was to pass the GED test and go to college.

In Congo, after about 16 years of wandering in low paying jobs, Gilbert, an old schoolmate, finally decided to go back to school and prepare for his State Diploma, which he successfully passed in 1998. Gilbert can now participate in a meaningful debate among other educated folks of his community. Now, Gilbert has a reason for a finer smile because he has accomplished a great deal by furthering his education. Between 1989 and 1992, some of my adult students in Cameroon became my close friends. They were working adults who enrolled in the after-school programs and were determined to break the pedal of illiteracy.

By helping our adult population with basic reading and writing, African governments would have achieved one of the major goals. Hopefully, people would read newspapers, articles of the constitution, and road maps and billboard signs for themselves; they would read petitions that they are often asked to sign by unpleasant politicians who want their votes during electoral campaigns.

Literacy also comes with its share of responsibilities; that means citizens could become more responsible in carrying out their duties and accomplish a little bit more in the effort to develop their own communities, provinces, and countries. Literacy could also improve people's lives by enabling them to get better jobs that would eventually raise their wages, and every increased pay could mean more buying power and more taxes for the treasury department. Literacy can indeed reduce several health-related issues, such as basic hygiene. Reading and understanding simple instructions on a medical prescription or the ability to follow doctor's written recommendations could well prevent certain unforeseen health risks.

Lack of education is costly, indeed. For example, with poor living conditions, the average person in Africa would rather spend less money on cheap drugs, which are often improperly stored and sometimes expired. Commonly, single usage needles have been reused by hospitals that cannot afford to purchase new ones. According to *Literacy Advocate*, a private nonprofit literacy organization whose mission and purpose is to sponsor educational programs and empower adults and their families, International Partners does promote literacy as a tool for social change. "ProLiteracy Worldwide" mentions some of the successful literacy programs that are already making an impact in Latin America and other places around the world. For instance, *AYUDA MUTUA* is a literacy program that promotes health, human rights, environmental actions, and micro-business in Mexico. In Haiti, *FLORESTA* advocates literacy, health, and agriculture among hundreds of rural families near Jacmel. In Peru, *SOROPTIMIST-TRUJILLO* focuses on teaching women basic reading and writing skills in the impoverished rural zone near Trujillo.[32] Not only will literacy benefit an individual, but it will also affect his or her community in a meaningful way.

Literacy builds up a person and it ensures self-esteem. When individuals are confident in themselves, they are likely to communicate better, to meet the challenges of life, and to become models for others. Thus, helping Africa become literate should be the focus of every African government. This kind of help must begin within the family nucleus, then within the local church, mosque, government, and hopefully with the support of international agencies that are willing to contribute.

Though literacy programs come with some challenges, it is possible that these programs will succeed once people are determined

---

[32] *ProLiteracy Publication Worldwide*, Summer 2003, 1.

to meet the challenges. We believe that it is time for African governments to encourage a more active partnership towards literacy programs. This partnership should involve local businesses and other institutions such as local profit and non-profit organizations, churches, high schools, community colleges, etc.

In Europe and the United States, businesses involved in promoting educational and social programs are often eligible for tax breaks and other privileges. In the United States, according to *LitScape*, a publication of ProLiteracy America Summer 2003, Verizon Wireless, one of the leading wireless communication companies, sponsors literacy programs through its Verizon Literacy University, which is the world's first online university dedicated to literacy. V.L.U. was formally launched in May 2003 in New York City.[33]

In another study, Namibia and the Crisis of Constructive Engagement, Robert I. Rotberg suggests that a leadership without character can easily collapse. The lack of adequate personality can also become a major factor in the handling of life issues in any given society. Even though personalities differ, there must be in a general sense a common element in the interpretation of personality trait. In an attempt to define *personality*, Robert W. Leeper and Peter Madison make mention of several scenarios, which displayed different types of human personalities. Though they acknowledge how hard it may be to explicitly define the term personality, they think that personality is something within the person that makes him represent or perceive life situations as he does.[34]

This definition could be meaningful in a social ladder context where the powerful social class sees life situations from different lenses than the underprivileged class. It is also true that personality is a very complex concept. Whatever aspect of personality we deal with may only be a glimpse or an external assessment of an internal personality. When

---

[33] *LitScape*, A publication of ProLiteracy America, Summer 2003
[34] Robert W. Leeper & Peter Madison, *Toward Understanding Human Personalities*. (New York: Applet on-Century-Crofts, Inc. 1959),18.

chief Bilang thinks he understands Biffard's personality, he is only dealing with the external aspect of personality. Husbands may never fully grasp their wives' real personality because wives may only be displaying external personality. Both Bilang and Bifard were well known community leaders in the Badinga area in Congo. From a psycho therapeutic viewpoint, Leeper and Madison conclude that people do not frankly speak openly to others when it comes to personal matters. "Much of lives is covered by conventional veneer. We usually talk of relatively impersonal and external things-what we think about this or that, other person, what we have seen in this or that other book or movie, what the chances are that such and such a team will win."

A common aspect of people's external behavior can be seen in daily conversations. When James asks John how he is doing, John is quick to respond "fine" regardless of any problems he has in his life. This is mainly due to pride. And pride seems to be more prevalent in males than it is in females. When a male is hurting, he first tends to deny the ache. "I'm all right, I'm fine, or I'll be okay." This is a behavior that leaders often cultivate. They exhibit such behavior for the fear of being judged and for the discomfort of being exposed. In reality, some leaders tend to act upright until they are caught in wrongdoing. Even after being exposed, only a handful of them are willing to admit the misconduct. But many of them would rather cover up at first because they hate being embarrassed. In 1998, Bill Clinton, the former president of the United States of America, was extremely popular until his sexual misconduct with a White House intern became a public theme. In the United Kingdom, Prince Charles of Wales acted like everything in his marriage was fine until his secret love affair with Camilla Parker Bowles became known to the public. In 2007, French President Nicolas Sarkozy's uncovered divorce was like a shock to many observers. Consequently, it is fair to allude that occasionally a leader's inner personality does not truly reveal itself until the leader becomes honest and willing to open himself up. The majority of our African leaders behave as if their authority has always worked perfectly well, and their leadership has always been beyond reproach. In general, their tendency is to justify every course of action whether the results are credible or not.

It may sound preposterous to the African elite when we dare talk about retraining Africa's leadership in the 21st century. After all, Africa has produced enough leaders of its own in the last fifty years. There are now some reputable colleges and universities on the continent that have proven to be academically sound. According to InternetLab (Observatorio de Ciencia y Tecnología en Internet), edited by Fabio Sabatini of the University of Rome La Sapienza and University of Cassino, University of Cape Town, Universiteit Stellenbosch, Universiteit van Pretoria - University of Pretoria, American University in Cairo, University of Dar Es Salam, University of Zimbabwe, and University of Mauritius... are among the world's great universities. Some of the legendary world leaders have recently been African leaders.

However, the purpose of this chapter is not to overstate the greatness of the few African leaders who have emerged so far. Those leaders who have made an impact in Africa and elsewhere are only among the minority group anyway. And we thank these few legendary leaders who have set the tone for the future of Africa's leadership. I truly believe that the future of Africa lies on a high-quality leadership, a leadership committed to shake Africa's culture of the public administration. But to transition into a superior leadership, Africa's politics must face the reality of a collapsing leadership, as we know it today. We must humbly admit the failure of our leadership so that we are able to improve it by retraining ourselves. We must evaluate our leadership's path in the past and bring the needed change. By admitting our failure, we will open the door of learning from our previous mistakes and allow ourselves to retrain accordingly. We should never be ashamed or fear our failures and mistakes. Everyone makes mistakes and learns from them. According to *Business Week Online* of July 10, 2006, failure breeds success. Everyone fears failure, but breakthroughs depend on it. The best companies and people embrace their mistakes and learn from them.

COVER STORY PODCAST

"Ever heard of Choglit? How about OK Soda or Surge? Long after "New Coke" became nearly synonymous with innovation failure, these products joined Coca-Cola Co.'s (KO) graveyard of beverage busts."

"Failure is Part of Success."
- Nicholas Hall, serial entrepreneur, and founder of Start upfailures.com, says succeeding involves bouncing back and overcoming self-doubt.

To better grasp the implication of failure before the rule of success, we compiled several quotes about failure from some of the most successful and wealthiest people around the world.

"I have missed more than 9000 shots in my career. I have lost almost 300 games. On 26 occasions I have been entrusted to take the game winning shot and missed. And I have failed over and over and over again in my life. And that is why . . . I succeed."

Michael Jordan

"Failure should be our teacher, not our undertaker. Failure is delay, not defeat. It is a temporary detour, not a dead end. Failure is something we can avoid only by saying nothing, doing nothing, and being nothing."

Dr. Denis Waitley

"When one door closes another door opens; but we often look so long and so regretfully upon the closed door, that we do not see the ones which open for us."

Alexander Graham Bell

"Failure is the opportunity to begin again more intelligently."

Henry Ford

"The men who have done big things are those who were not afraid to attempt big things, who were not afraid to risk failure in order to gain success."

B.C. Forbes

"Someday I hope to enjoy enough of what the world calls success so that someone will ask me, "What's the secret of it?"

I shall say simply this: 'I get up when I fall down.'"

Paul Harvey

"Most successful people can identify one minute, one moment, where their lives changed, and it usually occurred in times of adversity."

Willie Jolley

"I think everyone should experience defeat at least once during their career. You learn a lot from it."

Lou Holtz

"When you are down on your back, if you can look up, you can get up."

Les Brown

"There are no failures - only feedback."

R. Bandler

"Failure is the path of least resistance."

Sir James Matthew Barrie

"If at first you don't succeed, think how many people you've made happy."

H. Duane Black

"Don't fear failure so much that you refuse to try new things. The saddest summary of a life contains three descriptions: could have, might have, and should have."

Louis E. Boone

"A minute's success pays the failure for years."

Robert Browning

"I'd rather be a failure in something that I love than a success in something that I hate."

George Burns

"A man may fail many times, but he isn't a failure until he begins to blame somebody else."

John Burroughs

"Men are failures, not because they are stupid, but because they are not sufficiently impassioned."

Struther Burt

"They never fail who die in a great cause."

George Gordon, Lord Byron

"Failure is the condiment that gives success its flavor."

Truman Capote

"Show me someone content with mediocrity and I'll show you someone destined for failure."

Johnetta Cole

"In order to succeed you must fail, so that you know what not to do the next time."

Anthony J. D'Angelo

"Defeat never comes to any man until he admits it."

Josephus Daniels

"The person who really thinks learns quite as much from his failures as from his successes."

John Dewey

"Show me a thoroughly satisfied man, and I will show you a failure."

Thomas Alva Edison

"I'm proof against that word failure. I've seen behind it. The only failure a man ought to fear is failure of cleaving to the purpose he sees to be best."

George Elliot

"The great dividing line between success and failure can be expressed in five words: "I did not have time."

Franklin Field

"Keep these concepts in mind: You've failed many times, although you don't remember. You fell down the first time you tried to walk. You almost drowned the first time you tried to swim . . . Don't worry about failure. My suggestion to each of you: Worry about the chances you miss when you don't even try."

Sherman Finesilver

"Failure is success if we learn from it."

Malcom S. Forbes

"A shy failure is nobler than an immodest success."

Kahlil Gibran

"Haste in every business brings failure."

Herodotus

"Before success comes in any man's life, he is sure to meet with much temporary defeat and, perhaps, some failures. When defeat overtakes a man, the easiest and most logical thing to do is to quit. That is exactly what the majority of men do."

Napoleon Hill

"There is no loneliness greater than the loneliness of a failure. The failure is a stranger in his own house."

Eric Hoffer

"When on the brink of complete discouragement, success is discerning that . . . the line between failure and success is so fine that often a single extra effort is all that is needed to bring victory out of defeat."

Elbert Green Hubbard

"There is no failure except in no longer trying. There is no defeat except from within, no really insurmountable barrier save our own inherent weakness of purpose."

Frank McKinney "Kin" Hubbard

"An inventor fails 999 times, and if he succeeds once, he's in. He treats his failures simply as practice shots."

Charles Franklin Kettering

"Failure is the foundation of success, and the means by which it is achieved."

Lao Tzu

"As the opportunity grows for unlimited growth and progress, the chances of failure increase. There is no such thing as a program that will provide security and growth and progress with no risk . . . even within the church. As freedom for unrestricted development is enhanced, the possibilities for failure are also increased. The risk factor is great."

Dean L. Larsen

"My great concern is not whether you have failed, but whether you are content with your failure."

Abraham Lincoln

"In great attempts it is glorious even to fail."

Vince Lombardi

"Because a fellow has failed once or twice, or a dozen times, you don't want to set him down as a failure till he's dead or loses his courage - and that's the same thing."

George Horace Lorimer

"Remember the two benefits of failure. First, if you do fail, you learn what doesn't work; and second, the failure gives you the opportunity to try a new approach."

Roger Von Oech

"What we call failure is not the falling down, but the staying down."

Mary Pickford

"If we don't succeed, we run the risk of failure."

Dan Quayle

"I've come to believe that all my past failure and frustrations were actually laying the foundation for the understandings that have created the new level of living I now enjoy."

Anthony (Tony) Robbins

"Failure is not a single, cataclysmic event. You don't fail overnight. Instead, failure is a few errors in judgment, repeated every day."

Jim Rohn

"Success is never ending: failure is never final."

Robert Schuller

"You may be disappointed if you fail, but you are doomed if you don't try."

Beverly Sills

"The saddest failures in life are those that come from not putting forth the power and will to succeed."

Edwin Percy Welles

"I would rather lose in a cause that I know some day will triumph than to triumph in a cause that I know some day will fail."

Wendell Wilkie

"Defeat is not the worst of failures. Not to have tried is the true failure."

George E. Woodberry

"No one can defeat us unless we first defeat ourselves."

Dwight Eisenhower

"It is not the great temptations that ruin us; it is the little ones."

John W. DeForest

The concept of leadership is crucial to every human society and must therefore be understood properly. A community without leadership resembles a ship without a captain, a classroom without a teacher often leads to chaos, and a home without the headship of a father or mother will fall into desolation. Leadership is important because it empowers both the leader and the followers. Leadership does affect people's lives one way or the other.

To better comprehend the role of leadership, we turned our attention to some of the leadership scholars who possess expertise in leadership. Some have published books and articles, and others have held seminars and conferences worldwide. John C. Maxwell, a senior pastor at Skyline Wesleyan Church in California, is considered the most influential leader of his denomination.

He minimally defines leadership as influence. Even though he admits that he can count more than fifty ways of defining the term, "Leadership is influence," he said.[35]

This definition can be true in the sense that every leader influences people one way or the other. A good leader will influence positively while a bad one will influence negatively. My father's character and sense of integrity has affected me positively because of the positive influence he had on me. On the other hand, uncle Miye's

---

[35] Maxwell, John C.: *Developing the Leader Within You*, (Nashville: Thomas Nelson Publishers, 1993), 1.

poor character did affect me at one point of my life because of the negative influence it had on me.

Africa needs leaders who can influence positively. As Maxwell indicated, this is not about positional leadership, nor experiential leadership, but leading leadership and expertise leadership. In other words, a leader is not necessarily the boss, but that one who is able to influence other people. Every person has the potential to influence others, but not everyone influences.

Our intent is nothing but to stress the need for a positive leadership in Africa, which I call here *Impact Leadership*. This kind of leadership ought to be institutionalized and taught at all levels. One way to promote this impact leadership is to redesign our instructional curriculum so that our children are taught the essentials of leadership skills at a very early stage of their life. Education can be one of the best channels to revolutionize the entire society. The lessons that children learn well from going to school stick better than anything else. Students at this early age often come home defending their teachers, and they do this because they believe in their teachers so much.

In a decent environment, teachers are perceived as role models. Any parents with school-aged children can attest to this. Children would almost cry whenever their parents make a negative remark about their teachers. In fact, smart parents know that you cannot easily undo what a teacher has taught. Because of their *blank slate* state of mind, children are unable to make a good judgment. Even when a teacher makes an error, students still think that the teacher is right. That is why John Locke, the British philosopher, compares a child's brain to a blank slate in his *Tabula Rasa* educational theory. "The human mind is at birth a 'blank slate' without rule for processing data, and that data is added and rules for processing it formed solely by our sensory experiences".[36]

---

[36] John Locke, www.longlostlist.net/listforum/triage/Car_Incidents/ Index.htm, December 2007.

Once our children absorb the concept of leadership, they can then pass it onto their children and to the generations to come. It is hoped that, when this new generation graduates from high school and college, the concept of a positive leadership will have been established in their minds. Surely, this may take years of hard labor. But we must persist and persuade ourselves. We know that education is the catalyst of a society in many ways. But African school systems must carefully choose the kind of instruction and curriculum they will embrace because some of the curricula are not essentially designed for our schools. If the African school systems continue to depend on a western curriculum and instructional framework, it will be difficult for Africa to break through. However, education may also become a hindrance if we do not select the right kind of education that will truly meet the needs of our society. The war between *Traditional Education and Progressive Education* can only confuse our children. Many African school systems tend to embrace progressive education despite the hidden philosophy behind it.

According to the *Teacher-to-Teacher* pamphlet from Bob Jones University, not every secular textbook is appropriate for Christian schools. "Accusations of censorship... reveal the depth of philosophical problems inherent in the secular textbook industry.[37] In *"Is Public Education Necessary?"* Samuel L. Blumenfeld reveals the unseen agenda of progressive Education. He thinks that Progressive Education is the result of the anti-God movement trying to replace truth by relativism. Blumenfeld criticizes Robert Owen's opposition to God and religion. "The key dogma in Robert Owen's system was the notion that man's character had been deformed by religious brain washing and that only 'rational' education could correct it."[38]

In Africa, our school systems and governments can use positive

---

[37] Dawn L. Watkins, editor. *Teacher to Teacher: Balanced Perspectives in Education*, BJU Press, vol. 11, no 5, Dec. 2007.

[38] Samuel L. Blumenfeld, Is Public Education Necessary? Boise: The Paradigm Company, 1981, 72.

education as a channel to change the African society. Parents and educators should work together to bring this change. Likely, a responsible leadership will generate a responsible behavior. When a leader is responsible enough in a small scope, he or she will likely be responsible enough in a bigger capacity. Nevertheless, it takes more than just a mere theory of leadership to really materialize this concept of a good leadership. A good leader sets himself or herself apart from the bad apples by his or her character, vision, or unique personality. People can always tell the difference between a good chief and a bad chief by their ability to respond or react to difficult situations. Besides vision, character, and personality, a leader must be upright; humble; and accountable to God, to his followers, and to all his fellow men.

Chapter Seven

THE VISION FOR AN EFFECTIVE LEADERSHIP

A leader without a vision will lead his team into a pitfall. Without a vision, it becomes almost impossible to lead. In the Old Testament, prophet Isaiah plainly declares that without a vision, the people perish. It simply means that when leadership lacks a plan, not only the leader stumbles, but his followers and the entire society also pay the heavy price. This could be one reason why Africa is unstable and is still struggling in many areas. For the last fifty years, there have been countless military coups on the continent of Africa, an easier way to access into power.

Most of these self-imposed leaders usurp power and lack any kind of vision. Therefore, they develop a false sense of security because they struggle inwardly and outwardly. These leaders often build a fence of intolerance around them so that the citizens would give up their rights and refrain themselves from reacting against the bad policies the leaders put in place. Most of all, they fashion terror so that everyone can fear them. As a result, some have stayed in power longer than expected. Today, some of them who took power twenty years ago are still running the show and refuse to admit their failures. Most of them reject the idea of democracy or they fake it. Major Jimmi Wangome of the Kenyan army is one of the few African army officers who has spoken against military coups in the continent. He deplores the widespread use of military coups in Africa between 1960 and 1970, and slightly beyond. He writes, "Once coups started in Africa, they became like a wild African bushfire. They swept through the entire continent at an alarmingly high speed. They leapt through national borders as if those boundaries did not exist anymore."[39]

Vision in leadership is as fundamental as *planning* is to a builder. Imagine a builder without a plan to construct a home, an automobile manufacturer without a preset sketch, or a school system without guidelines for the entire school year. Although some people would argue that African leaders do have visions and plans, it is obvious that those visions and plans are obsolete. More than just mere visions, our biggest concern has been about putting in place better visions or better plans. In countries where leadership has been strong, governments have been effective, and the average population has reaped the benefits of their labor.

In the United States, vehicles, homes, or day-care facilities are well scrutinized before consumers access them. Any defects are immediately reported. Just in case some defects go unnoticed, companies will in many cases issue recalls so that the consumers are well protected. Such behaviors do not occur by chance or by the good will of the business owners. They are the results of good policies and laws put in place by a responsible government, a responsible legislature, and a responsible judiciary branch. And these branches of the government are often the repercussion of an effective visionary and a responsible leader. The logic is quite simple: Train people the right way and place outstanding individuals in leadership positions, and they will affect leadership in a positive way.

Another trend of leadership must gear towards transparency on the part of our leaders when it comes to speaking facts. Many times, when our leaders are confronted by tough questions from the media,

---

[39] Jimmi, Wangome. *Military Coups In Africa—The African "Neo Colonialism" That Is Self-Inflicted*, Kenya Army, CSC 1985. See internet, Dec. 16, 2006.

they tend to either become very nervous or try to hide the whole story. Some just avoid tough questions. In some African countries, the opposing newspapers, radios, or TV stations have simply been burned or destroyed because they criticize the government. This outrage has got to stop if Africa wants to become a true democracy.

In October 2006 on the French TV5 show "Grand Rendez-Vous", the president of the Republic of Congo, Denis Sassou Nguesso, also the then president of the African Union, was asked if the average person in his country benefited from the oil revenue that the country produces. He timidly said, "Yes." In reality, there are more people in Congo Brazzaville wishing they could live a decent life.[40] Careless answers like these can be very disturbing when those in leadership position cannot provide answers to easy questions without twisting the reality.

In *Developing "The Leader Within You,"* Maxwell provides some key qualities of a good leader. He devotes an entire chapter to vision. He mentions two crucial things that all great leaders possess: knowing where they are going and being able to persuade others to follow.[41] It is amazing how most of our leaders would fall into the influence of a negative leadership. By becoming something, they are not, their leadership becomes questionable. Sadly, many of our African leaders go into power to acquire wealth. They come in poor and hope to get out richer than anyone else. As a result, they intentionally allow a *laissez-faire* mentality around them so that their followers would leave them alone. Once the top leaders lead poorly, every follower catches the spirit of poor leadership, and the entire society is then infected.

One of the syndromes of poor African leadership is twofold: bribery and corruption. When leaders are involved in bribery and corruption, the entire system becomes contaminated, and no one is safe. In the book of Galatians, the Apostle Paul talks about the law of

---

[40] Grand Rendez-Vous "EUROPE 1-*TV5 MONDE-LE PARISIEN*, October 15, 2006.
[41] John, C. Maxwell, Ibid, 141

sowing and reaping. When top leaders in our nations offer illegal contracts to investors so that they can reap personal financial benefit, it is obvious that investors can operate as they please. In my college years, admission was supposed to be a free pass to all freshmen, yet most admission officers in many higher education institutions changed the rules by imposing fuzzy fees on new students. The faculty member could easily accept bribes from students who performed poorly on final exams. In a society like that, all that goes around comes around; there is no escape gate. The entire system will become corrupted, and whoever opposes the infected system is seen as an outsider. Then people become static and get used to the system that kills society slowly. That is why the concept of democracy, freedom of speech, or free elections in many parts of the continent does not have the same effect as it does elsewhere.

According to Maxwell, vision ranks very high in the quest for leadership. He defines vision as a clear picture of what the leader sees his or her group being or doing. I truly believe that leadership is about others, not just about *I, Me, My way, or Mine*. Without followers, there is no true leadership or there is none at all. On the other hand, when people follow without restraint, effective leadership takes place. In fact, in The Leadership Engine: How Winning Companies Build Leaders at Every Level, Noel M. Tichy, a professor at the University of Michigan Business School and a worldwide consultant specializing in leadership and organization transformation, confirms that successful leadership takes pride in developing other leaders. He talks about successful leaders having specific ideas, values, and experience to share goals through a clear vision. He writes, "The ultimate test for a leader is not whether he or she makes smart decisions and takes decisive action, but whether he or she teaches others to be leaders and builds an organization that can sustain its success even when he or she is not around." Even though Tichy speaks from the business point of view, these same principles he teaches can apply in politics, sports, economy, or any other field. But the biggest question we need to ask ourselves is whether our leaders have what it takes to build a successful leadership within and around themselves. How our leaders can become successful depends on how much they value their personal time versus office time; how they spend their personal money versus public funds; how they treat themselves versus how they treat others; and how they respond to personal crisis versus their response to the community or the nation's crisis. Successful leaders understand the need for time management. When a leader understands time management, he or she will plan his or her day wisely so that his daily agenda is filled with few interruptions.

Unfortunately, our leaders hardly believe in time management. The experience shows that our leaders do not believe in the idea of accountability, as if they do not have to answer to anyone under their leadership. Many of our leaders spend half of their time discussing personal matters, drinking Champaign, or chasing women. By the end of the day, not much is accomplished. In fact, they make their own schedule. Some get to work only around ten o'clock and leave at noon only to give instructions and sign critical documents, which they may or may not review carefully. Most of the leaders rely on their advisors yet are sometimes surprised to realize that their advisers mislead them. Regrettably, their slack behavior does affect some of the decisions they make routinely.

Because the future of a better Africa depends on a sound leadership, it is urgent that our leaders radically change their behavior. They must be willing to change and willing to take preventative actions that will enable Africa to stand up some day. In short, they must lead by example not by great speeches or good intentions. Dr. Lee Roberson, the late Founder and President Emeritus of Tennessee Temple University, often reminded his students and faculty members that "everything rises and falls on leadership."

Building our own infrastructure could be one of the accomplishments that African leadership needs to provide. Seldom are African leaders who receive medical treatment in their home hospitals because of the inadequacy of the health care system in place; many of them allow their children to study abroad because they no longer believe in their own educational system; athletes prefer to perform abroad because the working conditions and the dividends are far better than the ones at home and because their own countries do not value their talents; and the list goes on. Still, in the area of infrastructures, communication is another sector that needs improvement.

Someone once said that telecommunication between Kinshasa and Brazzaville was one of the most outrageous enigmas in Central Africa. While these two African capital cities, the closest in the world, sit face to face, their telephone connections must transit through France before these two sister cities can communicate with each other. And once the French telecommunication system breaks down, it will automatically paralyze these two African cities. We must not heavily depend on others.

Moreover, African people pay some of the highest airfares in the world because our transportation policies do not allow competitiveness. The one nation, one airline monopoly could be one of the reasons why airline fares are more expensive than the average person can afford. There is no reason why African airlines could not merge in order to allow competitiveness in their air space. And there is no reason why we cannot maintain a good health care system, manage a prosperous tourism industry, or provide a sound educational system rather than envying other nations' successes. We have shied away from the spirit of good competition. That is why even basic commodities become costly every day. From clean water to imported manufacturing goods, our people are paying an unbearable price. In addition, life expectancy is becoming shorter.

The Population of Sub-Saharan Africa in 2000

Population	Both Male & Female	Male	Female	Percentage
Under 5	110,883	55,910	54,973	17%
Under 5-15	290,982	146,434	144,548	44%
Working Age Pop. (15-64)	346,562	17,115	174,448	53%
Elderly (65+)	19,137	8,771	10,366	3%
Oldest Old (80+)	2,215	976	1,247	30%
Total	656,682	327,320	329,362	100%

See US Dept. of Commerce Economics & Statistics Administration/US Census Bureau 2002, 6.

Living a normal life has become a myth for most African children as if our children have been doomed to eternal suffering. There is no reason why foreign churches and international organizations should rescue our children for basic needs while our leaders and their children live bountifully. African leaders can develop strategies to manage the little resources they have. There are no real relief policies in place for most of our countries in case of unforeseen natural calamities. We often turn to rich nations to ask for help, yet we wonder why rich nations continue to shape and dictate our public policies.

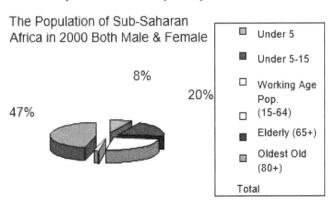

The Population of Sub-Saharan Africa in 2000 Both Male & Female

- Under 5
- Under 5-15
- Working Age Pop. (15-64)
- Elderly (65+)
- Oldest Old (80+)
- Total

Because of an unfortunate leadership and corruption in our countries, foreign governments and corporations find it easy to sign in cheap contracts in Africa. In many cases, most contracts benefit foreign investors to the detriment of Africa's economies. We must end our culture of total dependency on foreign aid. Africa can certainly create a more practical environment for a record prosperity for its people. But we must jointly take a stand for a new approach of conducting our businesses. We must go from the culture of begging to the culture of producing exceedingly. There is no reason why we cannot put in place a more responsible governing system, which will eradicate corruption so that we can attract more foreign investors.

When Africa sees corruption, nepotism, tribalism, or power struggle as a vice, perhaps civil wars will give way to a friendly dialogue and a peaceful environment. Money spent on guns to support the ideology of killing could well be spent where it is most needed. We must act smart and upright instead of complaining and blaming the West for all of our misery. We are in part liable and part of the problem to Africa's collapse.

Unless Africa's leadership changes its way of managing its administration and builds more responsible leaders now, it will continue to dangle. We can no longer wait for tomorrow. Today is it, and we must stop acting victimized. In his participant guide of *Today Matters*, John C. Maxwell emphasizes the need to make right decisions now. He believes that today's decisions will affect tomorrow's success. He furthermore discourages myths that we all create around success. Thus, he develops some of these disparities:

- "-Those who deem success is *impossible* will criticize it."
- "-Those who think success is *mystical* will search for it."
- "-Those who believe success comes from *luck* will hope for it."
- "-Those who feel success comes from *connection* will network.[42]"

[42] John, Maxwell C. *Today Matters: 12 Daily Practices To Guarantee Tomorrow's Success*, video 4-6. See Videos

As leaders, we must always measure the significance of the decisions we make today and how they will affect lives and communities around us tomorrow. Just as one good decision will make a huge positive impact, one bad decision will, on the other hand, have a negative impact as well.

In dealing with quality leadership, Professor Tichy continues to gain momentum. He suggests that sitting leaders should train more leaders to ensure continuity. He thinks that companies with the most leaders flourish more than those with few leaders. "The legacy of winning leaders is other leaders," he claims. Finally, he advises that sitting leaders give up their position when it is time to leave instead of trying to hang onto the position for life.[43] One reason why leaders who have been in power for a long time should train younger people is so that younger people with character, integrity, and vision can bring new dreams and a different style of leadership.

In today's fast changing world, many of our leaders of the old school simply do not get it. They should not always hang on to their past experience. Time has come for many of those leaders to retrain themselves or else quit. With the new technology and the venue of the worldwide web, dot-com, dot-org, dot-edu, electronic mails, ethernet, intranet… where businesses are routinely conducted online, it will be almost impossible to deny the fast pace the world has now embarked on. Many companies are now saving lots of money by simply asking some of their employees to work from the comfort of their homes.

In their book *"The Aprentice Hall of Directory of Online Business Information "(1997)*, Christopher Engholm and Scott Grimes suggest that the internet has become a rich source of business information, though it can sometimes be frustrating if users do not easily locate the needed data.[44] "Convergence is essentially changing the way we

---

[43] Noel, Tichy M. Ibid, 189.
[44] Christopher, Engholm & Scott Grimes. *The Apprentice Hall of Directory of Online Business Information 1997,* (Englewood Cliffs: Prentice Hall, 1996), 12.

communicate. Here we highlight how developments in the IT and telecoms businesses have made remote and flexible working a reality for many people.

Although the latest advances in mobile technology and the continuing growth in the adoption of broadband is enabling these practices to be implemented, smarter working is not just about technology: it is also about changing culture, and the way people work, and giving the skills to work smarter."

For the sake of convenience, time and money, many people now shop online. One can now even bank online, pay monthly bills, make travel arrangements, and so forth. In "The Internet Business Book," Jill H. Ellsworth & Matthew V. Ellsworth state principal reasons why businesses are using the internet. Among them they cite communication, corporate logistics, leveling the playing field, globalization, gaining and maintaining competitive advantage, cost containment, collaboration and development, information retrieval and utilization, marketing and sales, transmission of data, and creating a corporate presence.[45]

In 2005, my family had few deals online including the purchasing of travel insurance, airline tickets, and even Eurostar (the European Trans Train) tickets between London and Paris from the comfort of our home in Kennesaw, GA. In 2001, I had a shocking experience when a Compaq customer service agent was answering my questions all the way from Calcutta, India, after I had dialed the 1800 toll free number in the US. Many colleges and universities including lower grades now require professors, instructors, and teachers to use programs like WebCT to better interact with students. A few years ago, when I first became familiar with WebCT at the Community college where I worked as an Adjunct faculty, I thought it was a strange idea, but now, the idea has spread out to many more academic institutions. Some schools now use software such as Edline, a program

---

[45] Jill H. Ellsworth, & Matthew V. Ellsworth, *The Internet Business Book*, (New York: John Wiley & Sons, Inc., 1994), 31-32.

which enables parents to follow up their children's attendance and weekly progress. It would be needless to add that many colleges and universities have made it easier for students to take classes online.

Without a new vision and new set of mind or mentality in a changing world, Africa will continue to remain behind. Therefore, we must stand up and shake up the laws and the policies that impede progress. We must revolutionize our thought process; we must no longer tolerate a systematical poor leadership, which cannot provide radical changes. Susan Annunzio, the author of *eLeadership* and a partner at Nextera and assistant adjunct professor of management at the University of Chicago Graduate School of Business, talks about the eLeadership challenge, a world of global markets, ad hoc teams, telecommuters, emails, video conferences, online ordering, virtual offices, intranets, networked alliances, and instant information. She defines *eLeadership* as a new style of business management designed to specifically guide top executives as they retool their businesses to compete in the *eWorld*.[46]

The question of revolutionizing African leadership in the new millennium requires everyone's effort. We all can shape and reshape our leadership direction at all levels provided we develop a coherent and attainable plan with a clear vision. We also need to have courage and determination to place the deserving manpower where they can fully exercise their given expertise. The 21st century leaders can now better network with other leaders of the world without high costs, thanks to the wonder of the Internet.

---

[46] Susan, Annunzio. *ELeadership: Proven Techniques for Creating an environment of Speed and Flexibility in the Digital Economy*, (New York: The Free Press 2001), 11-12.

Chapter Eight
THE PERSONALITY OF A LEADER

When it comes to an exemplary leadership in Africa, look no further than Mandela's stereotype, because the man is the incarnation of Africa's leadership in its entirety. There is no doubt that Mandela represents the good side of leadership. In fact, his personality reflects leadership, and his vision confirms his leadership style. Despite the suffering he endured in prison, Mandela stayed tuned to his political principles, and he was always a source of strength to the other prisoners and to those who understood his fight for equality and fairness.

Born July 18, 1918, at Umtata, Cape of Good Hope, South Africa, Nelson Rolihlahla Mandela was in prison between 1962 and 1990. In 1994, he was elected as the very first black president in his native South Africa. The son of Chief Henry Mandela of the Xhosa-speaking Tembu people, Nelson Mandela renounced his claim to the chieftainship to become a lawyer. He attended the University College of Fort Hare and studied law at the University of Witwatersrand; he later passed the qualification exam to become a lawyer and in 1952 opened a firm with Oliver Tambo. In 1944, he joined the African National Congress (ANC), a black-liberation group, and in 1949 became one of its leaders, helping to revitalize the organization and opposing the apartheid policies of the ruling National Party.

Mandela went on trial for treason between 1956–61 but was acquitted. During the extended court proceedings, he divorced his first wife and married Nomzamo Winifred Madikizela (Winnie Madikizela-Mandela); they divorced in 1996.

After the massacre of unarmed Africans by police forces at Sharpeville in 1960 and the subsequent banning of the ANC, Mandela abandoned his nonviolent stance and began advocating acts of sabotage against the South African regime. In 1962 he was jailed and sentenced to five years in prison. In 1963 the imprisoned Mandela and several other men were tried for sabotage, treason, and violent conspiracy in the celebrated Rivonia Trial, named after a fashionable suburb of Johannesburg, where raiding police had discovered quantities of arms and equipment at the headquarters of the "Spear of the Nation," the ANC's military wing. Mandela had been a founder of the organization and admitted the truth of some of the charges that were made against him. On June 12, 1964, he was sentenced to life imprisonment.

From 1964 to 1982, Mandela was incarcerated at Robben Island Prison, off Cape Town. Mandela retained wide support among South Africa's black population, and his imprisonment became a celebrated cause among the international community that condemned apartheid. The South African government under President F.W. de Klerk released Mandela from prison on February 11, 1990. On March 2 Mandela was chosen deputy president of the ANC (the president, Tambo, being ill), and he replaced Tambo as president in July 1991. Mandela and de Klerk worked to end apartheid and brought about a peaceful transition to nonracial democracy in South Africa. In 1993 Mandela and de Klerk were awarded the Nobel Prize for Peace for their efforts.

As president, Mandela established the Truth and Reconciliation Commission (TRC), which investigated human rights violations under apartheid. In 1996 he oversaw the enactment of a new democratic constitution. The following year Mandela resigned his post with the ANC and in 1999 did not seek a second term as South African president.

After leaving office in June, he retired from active politics.[47] As a leader, Mandela has left a very good impression. He has inspired Africa and its populations. He has made history and deserves our respect. Mandela's example should enable Africa to produce more quality leaders.

Eugene E. Jennings, a professor at Graduate school of Business Administration at Michigan State University comments on the real personality of a leader. In his *Anatomy of Leadership: Princes, Heroes, and Supermen*, he talks about the rebirth of the leader; he wonders if some leaders who perform poorly have not become insufficient in their ability to lead, and that, if they still hold up into their leadership position, it is because they now depend on external resources.[48] Such resources could be the invested power and authority they have received, the prestige associated with the function they exercise, the immune status they have been granted by their constitutions.

Professor Jennings' remarks simply coincide with our previous assessment on African leadership as a whole. There seems to be more evidence attesting to the fact that some of our leaders are just unfit to lead consistently. Some heads of states have clung to power for more than thirty years leaving no legacy but chaos. Yet, they continue to run for office repeatedly. The fact that they have become less popular does not concern them. Elsewhere, such leaders would have been thrown out in no time. If one cannot do well in the first two consecutive terms, then one should look for another job or leave the seat to more competent candidates.

In many African countries today, their newly amended constitutions only allow two consecutive terms at the presidency; but some dictators have been swift enough to amend the constitution to make it meet their selfish desire to remain in power much longer. They try very hard to defend their poor records, and they sometimes fabricate electoral procedures, which in most cases favor them.

---

[47] *Encyclopædia Britannica* Online. 9 Mar. 2008 <http://www.britannica.com/eb/article

[48] Eugene E. Jenning, *An Anatomy of Leadership: Princes, Heroes, and Supermen*, (McGraw-Hillbook, NY: 1960), 221.

Furthermore, the dictators passionately rely on their tribal and ethnic support system, which often causes divisions and unnecessary conflicts among the people. A few examples are Chad, Zimbabwe, Gabon, Cameroon, and Kenya. On the other hand, other heads of states have mightily relied on foreign diplomacy, army, and various resources. They have simply ignored their populations because they feel obligated to serve their masters who do provide them with funds, weapons, and other aids. Such leaders do not mind at all brutalizing or torturing those who dare question their records of mismanagement. In Africa, many front-runner journalists have paid the ultimate price for trying to speak out.

Robert Greenleaf, known for his writing on power ethics, management, organizations, and servanthood, stresses the need for preparedness. According to him, a leader who wants to make a difference must take time to prepare himself even before he takes the leadership position. "Maybe this is why so many who occupy seats of power seem so old when they are not really old. They are simply not prepared for the leadership that would take their institution beyond success ..."[49] Then Greenleaf adds, "Ambition is a great thing when the primary goal is growth of the person." American voters can well attest to this since they are aware of the electoral process, and they know many of the candidates who stopover in the Whitehouse in Washington, DC. In 1992 and 2000, both Bill J. Clinton and George W. Bush were sworn in as young men with darker hair, yet they came out older with lots of gray hair and facial wrinkles. Being prepared takes time and sometimes it can be a lengthy process. It took Joseph, Moses, and Joshua several years of preparedness before they became effective leaders. It is first a matter of gathering the central elements of the future change. Being prepared has a lot to do with planning; it is about developing self-discipline, and it is also about building a favorable thought process. Most of all, it is about submitting every stage of the leadership process to God and letting Him grant wisdom

---

[49] Robert K. Greenleaf, *On Becoming A Servant Leader*, (Jossey-Bass Publishers: 1996), 264.

for a steady leadership. God does not want us to turn to Him only after we mess up. In fact, He wants us to turn to Him even before trouble comes. God wants our success, that is why He expects us to hand Him the wheel of our leadership.

Sadly, many leaders, especially African leaders, often bypass this preparedness stage. They are in a rush to occupy a leadership position with or without any formal training or experience. Since 1960, many of them have refused to acknowledge their failures. Therefore, they have created an external and protective mechanism, which secures their right to command. Some have built squadrons for their personal protection. Others have built personal wealth, which enables them to bribe and corrupt their followers including their opponents. Without an adequate preparation for the African leadership, the black continent will continue to deteriorate politically, economically, and socially. That is why we share John D. Adams' view of transformational leadership as well. In his *Transforming Leadership: from vision to results*, Adams encourages leaders to embrace the concept of participatory management that is involving other people in the leadership process.[50] Because leadership is a shared responsibility, the top leader must learn to delegate power instead of conserving it. This way, much is accomplished in less time. That is simply the power of wisdom: "Two are better than one." Thus, creative and intuitive leadership where problems and decisions are made in a much broader and deeper context is the way to go according to Adams. When leaders are prepared, they will likely plan well and focus their energy towards a common goal for the benefit of their populations. Prepared leaders know how to plan, and quite often they receive a higher mark of respect from their people; they seem to have confidence in the process of making their decisions; they equally weigh the pros and the cons before decisions are made.

---

[50] John D. Adams, *Transforming Leadership: From Vision to Results.* Miles River Press, (Alexander: 1986), 105-106.

Chapter Nine

A POSITIVE CHANGE IN LEADERSHIP ROLE

There is no secret that sometimes in our journey in life, we have been exposed to the temptation of resisting change. I grew up in a small community where the main food was *Kwanga (a vegetable root similar to the Cuban Yuca)*. Once out of the area, I was almost forced to change my diet to a different kind of meal. To be honest, *Fufu (Kwanga flour)* was never part of our family diet except when there was no other choice. At first, it did not make sense why some tribes around Idiofa and Kikwit would prefer *Fufu* to *Kwanga*. So, I resisted that change. In the last few years many changes have occurred in my personal life. Some changes have been wonderful and some others disastrous. At first, it always appears that change is inconsistent with mankind's comfort zone. We like the repetitive course of action; we cherish the same brand of behavior, and we enjoy doing the same things over and over. We have even bought into a theory that if the system works, do not try to change it; or why re-invent the wheel when the first wheel still performs well. Once again, the English popular saying: "If it is not broken, do not fix". Such reasoning is simply consistent with the theory of resisting change. When Microsoft upgrades its operating systems from Windows 95 to

Windows 2000 then to Windows Vista, we first tend to hate the change. But once we become accustomed to the systems, our whole attitude about change varies. We know that change occurs in every line of business we do, including politics. When the expected results are not plausible, we must find ways to improve our production. And this can only happen through a positive change. When coaches notice that players are not scoring, they become very agitated and anxious. They coach players to modify their techniques. Sometimes, they scream loud and even yell at players hoping that players will do better so that they can score and win the game.

At the beginning of Fall 2007, I had the privilege to coach the girls' soccer team at Miami Christian School. My desire or motivation was to see my team win every game. We trained with a motivation to win all our games. As leaders, we should always have the same mindset and the same desire athletic coaches have: the "Play to win" concept. In any sport, the results matter. What a beautiful thing if African politicians would adopt the same kind of frame of mind. Our Presidents, governors, and CEOs should really manage their governments and other institutions like a good football or soccer team with a distinctive desire to win. Once, they realize that their governments are not achieving the expected results, they ought to bring the needed change.

Berrett Koelher insists that change in leadership is necessary and healthy. She refers to Sir Isaac Newton, the British physicist, mathematician, astronomer, natural philosopher, and chemist who stunned the scientific world with his universal law of gravitation and the three laws of motion in 1687." The new sciences are filled with tantalizing and hopeful processes that foster change. But to learn these lessons, we need to shift what we look for."[51]

In her book *Doing Leadership Differently: Gender, Power and Sexuality in a Changing Business Culture*, Amanda Sinclair provides some strategies used by women to influence. She mentions:

[51] Margaret J. Wheatley, *Leadership and the New Science (Discovering Order in a Chaotic World)*, (Berrett-Koelher Publishers, Inc.: San Francisco 2006), 139.

- An outreach both upward and across the aisles (to superiors, peers, and clients)
- Submerging ego (eg. Giving others the opportunity to decide)
- Being a confidant (safe and trusted ally, good listener)
- Seeking advice and creating a network (building up contacts outside your business)
- Defining boundaries[52]

Sinclair is right when she develops these strategies of good character, humility, integrity, and accountability, which we must rely on. Our leaders should never take their headship for granted because they are called to serve their people and not to be served as we see it often today.

As for Ulf Engel, a political scientist, and Associate Professor of politics in Africa at the Institute of African Studies at the University of Leipzig and Gorm Rye Olsen, a political scientist as well and head of the Department for European Studies at the Danish Institute for International Studies point out in a very straight forward manner the wrong path that African politics is following at the beginning of this twenty-first century. In their introduction, they show how developing continents like Asia and Latin America are achieving some progress in governance. They see the entire African continent still struggling with good governance. We must agree with these two experts that Africa is still trailing. These two professors understand the fundamentals of good governance and they are providing Africa with some compelling insights. One of the reasons why there is bad governance in the continent of Africa is because of the lack of a strong leadership. "More than a decade after the end of the Cold War and the second wind of change, many of Africa's political systems at best resemble façade democracies."[53]

---

[52] Amanda Sinclair, *Doing Leadership Differently: Gender, Power and Sexuality in a Changing Business Culture*, (Melbourne University Press, 2005), 113-114.
[53] Ulf Engel & Gorm Rye Olsen, *The African Exception*, (University of Leipzig 2004), 1.

In Political Leadership in Africa, John Cartwright argues that not all leaders exercise leadership. This argument coincides with our earlier position about the natural leadership. It is like a person dressing up like a professional hunter. Despite the camouflage, one does not just become a professional hunter simply by putting on the outfit. It takes great skills and years of hunting experience and tactics to become a skillful hunter. Many politicians in a leadership position have worked their way up, but the end results have not been great. Thus, Cartwright writes, "It is no accident that all these illustrations of leadership do share the ability of a leader to act, rather than being the passive beneficiary of the events. Leadership clearly involves the leader doing something, something that wins support from followers. Yet not all leaders exercise leadership."[54]

In the next few lines, we would like to emphasize again that this argument reflects our view that leadership is not a mere application of a learned sets of rules. Contrary to the popular belief that everyone is born to lead, we sustain the natural leadership theory, which is by far God's empowerment and gift from above. How do I explain to my students Moses' ability to lead the nation of Israel when he had never had any course on effective leadership? How did the little David conquer the Philistines and scare King Saul when he had never been exposed to any principles of Leadership 101 before? The Bible is full of illustrations concerning effective leadership under God's guidance. When God empowers a person to lead, even the weakest person of all, the dynamics of leadership will change. Yes, there exists a natural leadership. That is why we see the difference between those who force themselves into becoming leaders and those who are called to lead. In the New Testament when Jesus reached out to the common people of his days, He empowered them. Ordinary people like Peter, Thomas, Simon, and many others were able to accomplish exceedingly. Jesus saw in them a God-given gift or the natural gift in

---

[54] John Cartwright, *Political Leadership in Africa*, (St. Martin Press, Inc., 1983 NY), 20.

them. Throughout the world, natural born leaders have left their prints; although they have been gone for a while, their legacy and philosophy still affect the world. There have been more positive reflections from the natural born leaders than from those who invested themselves into an artificial leadership. The difference between natural and artificial leadership is that the natural leader is usually called whereas the artificial leader appoints himself. The natural leader listens more than he talks, while the artificial leader commands more than he listens. The natural leader takes advice, but the artificial leader rejects advice because he likes to dictate.

As stated earlier, Africa has had some of the talented world leaders in the past. That is why it is crucial that the actual leaders who are not performing well evaluate themselves. They must have the courage to relinquish power to others for the benefit of the entire continent. When we talk about leadership collapse, we mean at every level of governmental institutions. John W. Harbeson and Donald Rothchild are two editors who have identified some of the problems that face the black continent. In their book entitled *Africa in World Politics: The African State in Flux* published at Westview in 2000 in Boulder, they see Africa's future dwindling if nothing major is done to stop the capsizing of the continent. They mention their contributor Thomas M. Callaghy who wrote, "At the dawn of the twenty-first century, Africa must quickly elect the path it wishes to follow. On the one hand, it could allow the forces of implosion and ethnic warfare to become the masters of its fate, to the advantage of a few potentates lacking vision or warlords with transient alliances. Thus, history would repeat itself, with the suffering that this entails, and this old continent would be at the mercy of all types of corruption" (43).

In chapter 4 of his book and in an attempt to define African leadership, Jacob U. Gordon wanted to establish the concept of the foundations of African leadership. While Gordon is right for believing that the foundations of African leadership are deeply rooted in African cosmology and worldview, we disagree with his idea of the corrupted

African leadership, which has proved its limitations. By emphasizing elements like ageism, tribalism, or kinship, the argument may be misleading for the simple reason that there has been a big gap between the respected traditional African leadership and the neo-corrupted leadership as seen today. As we mentioned in the previous chapters, the ancient Africa had its style of leadership, which by no means can be compared to the present bankrupt leadership. Once, the ancient Africa had developed a unified, organized, and dignified leadership where kings and emperors recognized their boundaries. There were mutual agreements as to whom this or that portion of the land belonged. In their diversities, the ancestral powers led their populations in the right directions. Yes, there were conflicts and divisions, but those conflicts and divisions were never as tumultuous and costly as we see them today. The concept of the corruption Africa is being accused of today never reached a high proportion like we see it nowadays. Someone ought to be brave enough to accept the blame for the breakdown of African leadership. That is why we appeal to our generational leaders to meet the challenge of the African leadership in this twenty-first century. However, Gordon brings some positive thoughts to why the African leadership got into the shape it has been in. He writes, "The important aspect of the African leadership foundation is the impact of colonialism in Africa. The colonial legacies, the introduction, and imposition of European values and institutions on Africa as part of colonial policies have had a tremendous impact on African leadership."[55] [56]

When dealing with the concept of leadership in Africa, one must break through the minds of African culture to truly understand why many leaders in Africa act the way they do. In our quest to better catch the meaning of leadership according to Africa's establishment, we launched a survey among the African elite from all walks of life. The

---

[55] Jacob U. Gordon, *African Leadership In The Twentieth Century: An Enduring Experiment In Democracy* (University Press of America, NY 2002), 155.
[56] Jacob U. Gordon, *Ibid*, 169.

survey consisted of two main thoughts: the definition of leadership and its significance in the African context.

After reviewing the answers from our survey, we finally came to appreciate the real sense of leadership according to the African mind. Leadership in Africa seems to have been confused with autocracy. Almost at every level of leadership, people tend to perform in a tyrannical manner. Whether leadership is at lower or higher scale, our behavior can easily alter. Leaders seem to want more power, and they tend to dominate the debate. In middle school, I was once appointed as the class captain; unfortunately, I expected a lot from my classmates, and I simply acted like the boss on several occasions. Because my classmates did not know any better, they appeared to tolerate my authoritarian attitude at that time. At school, some of my teachers had the same attitude. You could never win an argument against your teacher just because of the boss-like mentality, which overwhelmed them; the principal would often believe that a teacher must always be right. In almost every sector, those in charge would be inclined to act arrogantly. A supervisor would easily win an argument against his down line crew member, a policeman or an armed forces officer would always win against a civilian; not to mention an adult versus a minor person, or a man versus a woman. In the community where I grew up, the foreman of the community expected to be always served. In many cases, he received the best share whether he took part in the hunting activity or not. With the same mindset, the chief could marry as many wives as he wished because he did not have to answer to anybody.

Behind the notion of cultural leadership lies the concept of family and ethnic web, a complex network made of uncles, aunts, cousins, nephews, and nieces. It is a concept in which everyone is part of the growing family. And being part of this family network, one would simply assume that every person in this network would expect a special treat whether they qualify for something or not. Once the chief in charge in the community sees the need to appoint a follower, he would first like to choose the appointee within his close or extended family. Competencies do not really matter anymore as far as public service is concerned.

One writer who confirms our thought about the wrong idea of extended family is B n zet Bujo, who comments on the difference between Western thinking and African thinking. Bujo fundamentally advocates African ethics in terms of community contrary to the European or American ethics. He comments, "As I have said, the community has a central place in African ethics. It must be emphasized that this ethics is not the product of the western rationality with which we are familiar (as in Descartes or Kant), where discursive reason is central."[57]

Therefore, the real question now is about what style of leadership Africa should implement: a conventional leadership, which has led to unprecedented success worldwide, or the cultural and unconventional leadership, which Africa has embraced so far. Because of Africa's unpleasant experience in the area of cultural leadership, we henceforward disagree with the idea of cultural leadership, which has sadly been founded on favoritism, bribery, traffic of power and influence.

If this kind of leadership does not improve, Africa will continue to plunge drastically into the abyss of helplessness. According to the United Nations site for the Millennium Development Goals Indicators updated in 2007, Africa is still trailing due to lack of progress in many phases of the global development. "At the midway point between their adoption in 2000 and the 2005 target date for achieving the Millennium Development Goals, sub-Saharan Africa is not on track to achieve any of the Goals."[58]

---

[57] Bēnēzet Bujo, *Foundations of An African Ethic: Beyond the Universal Claims of Western Morality*, The Crossroad Publishing Co., NY 2001), 3.
[58] UN Statistics Division, Dept. of Economic & Social Affairs, 20 June 2007.

Chapter Ten

THE MORAL CHARACTER OF
A LEADER

Moral character may be one of the most difficult things to comprehend. The need for moral integrity in leadership ought to become an essential component in African political affairs. It is apparent that the bankrupt leadership in Africa results essentially from the lack of moral character and integrity from many of our leaders. Many African leaders produce beautiful speeches, yet they are in many respects inconsistent with their actions. They say one thing in the morning but do another one in the evening. Some are better known through justifying every mistake they make. They behave as if they are self-righteous.

Many say good things about character, many teach it, and many think about it. However, they cannot deliver the kind of moral integrity that only God provides. Schools, churches, synagogues, and mosques have taught it and continue to teach it, but it does not always produce good results because they do it their way. Until man goes back to the source of moral integrity, not much will be accomplished.

Unfortunately, man tries very hard to solve his own set of problems his own way because he wants to always be in charge. He pushes God aside and expects God to answer positively. For centuries, despite a great deal of progress in our world today, things do not seem better for mankind. The quest for answers to life's fundamental questions continues to haunt man's mind. The same conflict between good and evil, which disrupted life in the Beautiful Garden, continues to divide mankind today—The concept of life and death, the two contradictory worldviews: humanism versus Christianism, absolutism versus relativism, and so forth. In 1859 when Charles Darwin came up with his species theory of evolution, atheists and a certain scientific academia claimed victory. Decades later, we still debate about the accuracy of the concept of the origin of mankind.

The character factor in the public sector is declining considerably. The wrong choices we make today are the reason why moral integrity no longer matters. Because we dislike absolute values in our lives, the repercussions can be felt almost everywhere whether we deny the fact or not. From our schools to the workplace, we fight the necessary values, only to replace them with provisional ones. "Every age and every people have a character stamped upon it by the heroes and visions it honors." (Charles E. Watson)[59]

Does character matter in leadership, one may wonder? In fact, we believe that character must be one of the primary prerequisites in the leadership role. Without a shadow of doubt, character in leadership not only sets a good tone but also carries the leader further than expected. A good character shapes even bad leaders because good character is a virtue. Frank Harmick explains character from the Greek and Latin root. He says that character refers to an engraving instrument. It has to do with a distinctive engraving or marking made on one's pattern of behavior, moral strength, or personal qualities,[60] Harmick added.

A good character forges leaders to become mindful of every action they take and decisions they make. It helps them see the future with promising lenses; it builds a good rapport between them and

---

[59] Charles E. Watson, *Managing With Integrity: Insights from America's CEOs*, Praeger New York 1991, 3.

[60] Frank Harmick, *Proverbs: The Fountain of Life* (Positive Action, Whitakers 1999), 135.

their followers; it causes positive changes, and it brings stability, peace, security, and consecration. But how can African leaders develop character, if many of them have not been exposed to it?

Because character is contagious, we must teach it and strive to live it as well. Our schools must develop moral and ethical curricula, which will spring into all the school systems across Africa so that our children are taught good principles of life right at the early stage of their lives. But children must also experience moral character at home. How then can homes provide this virtue if they have never received any in the first place? That is why we encourage churches and mosques to get more involved in helping homes develop good character. The home, being the foundation of all institutions, has a key role to play in the make-up of a society. Our governments ought to support the effort of the clergy in building good character among citizens. In other words, governments should mobilize necessary funds to help churches, synagogues, and mosques reach this goal because it is the noble thing to do.

Leadership is well achieved when it becomes a shared responsibility. Therefore, African governments should create a mechanism for the clergy to play a role in the moral leadership of their converts. Moral character brings more than just a wealth of devotion, but also a sense of responsibility, peace and stability. It couples with integrity and many other good qualities of life.

In Managing with Integrity: Insights from America's CEOs, Charles E. Watson makes a good point: "There is wholeness in what the person with integrity says and does. There is consistency between his actions and what he purports to honor."[61]

But we know that true character originates from truth and truth comes from God alone, and it is also known as absolute truth. On our own, we may obtain moral and ethical character, which will keep us running; however, with true character from God, man will value himself, then value others. There will be fewer conflicts and more

---

[61] Charles E. Watson, *Ibid*, 171.

occurrences of love and peace, and the world will experience the power of moral character and its benefits. In short, the right kind of moral and ethical character will make us achieve even more.

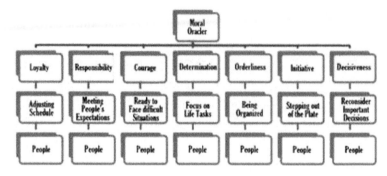

The Character Chart

In Character Sketches from the Pages of Scripture, Rand McNally breaks down the different components of good character. He mentions loyalty, responsibility, courage, determination, orderliness, initiative, and decisiveness.

- *Loyalty:* the leader will learn to adjust his schedule, stand besides needy people, be a reliable messenger, know and follow the wishes of the people he or she serves.
- *Responsibility:* the leader will strive to meet people's expectations, realize the importance of his or her tasks and complete them, then turn regular tasks into enjoyable experiences.
- *Courage:* the leader should be ready to face difficult situations, follow instructions in the face of danger, apply available resources in a creative way, and confront the opponent or enemy with confidence that will ultimately succeed.
- *Determination:* the leader needs to understand that today's struggles are necessary for future achievement, concentrate on achievable goals, expand his or her energy to complete

essential tasks, reject any possible distractions.

- *Orderliness:* the leader must be organized by maintaining cleanliness and good grooming, by removing items that could hinder achievement.
- *Initiative,* the leader will expand his world by exploring new areas of interest for his people. He is expected to take the lead to relieve pressure from those around him or her. He or she will act with confidence by responding quickly and wisely to challenging situations.
- *Decisiveness:* the leader ought not to reconsider an important decision, which he or she thinks is right to the best interest of the people. He or she must avoid future failures by devoting his or her energy to the right course of action and by evaluating this course of action quickly and accurately.[62]

Manfred F. R. Kets de Vries defines character as the sum of the deeply ingrained patterns of behavior that defines an individual. He further establishes the connective progression among the principal elements that form character. Thus, he states that our thoughts usually become our actions, our actions lead to habits, our habits become our character and our character will become our destiny here on earth.[63]

Is it possible to talk about leadership without ethics? Or is it even possible to discuss success in leadership in the absence of sound morality and character? One thing leaders should do is to check out their own records both private and public in the course of their terms in the office. Leaders' performance is based on how well they are willing to evaluate themselves. Self-evaluation brings an edge of trust, confidence, and humility into future actions. When leaders evaluate

---

[62] Rand McNally, Character, Sketches from the Pages of Scripture, (Rand McNally & Co. 1978), TC
[63] Manfred F. R. Kets de Vries, *The Leader on the Couch*, (Jossey-Bass, West Sussex 2006), 52

themselves with a pure heart, they are likely to see their failures. And from failures, they will likely come out stronger because they know where they have stumbled, and they are likely to avoid past mistakes. That is why Terry L. Price wants everyone to understand ethical failures in leadership today. In his introduction, Price charges leaders with a behavior common to all the world leaders.

However, African leaders at all levels more often display this common behavior. "... leaders think that they are special, that ordinary rules do not apply to them, and that followers should do as the leader says, not as the leader does."[64] Well the truth of the matter is that people care less about what their leaders say concerning rules and regulations; rather they care more about how well their leaders keep up with these rules and regulations.

When Price talks about failures in leadership, he does not only see the wrong desire, the bad motives, or the self-centeredness of the leader; he also sees the volitional and cognitive sides within the leader. This may well explain our argument in favor of natural leadership, which suffers less from volition and cognition. Is it possible that the failure in Africa's leadership has suffered terribly from the volitional or cognitive account? If the answer is yes, we then desperately need a supernatural help before we can emerge. The naturally born leadership may be the route Africa should follow.

One way a naturally born leader reacts to criticism is to carefully listen to his critics and pay attention to their requests if they are founded and if they meet the best interest of the people. A naturally born leader also puts the interest of his people first. He or she listens to the people he or she represents. On the other hand, we know what most political leaders want when they are out there campaigning for a position. This is the moment many politicians become more friendly and even generous by offering gifts, money, and gratis services. Almost all speeches tend to place the voters in a ranking position. About every

---

[64] Terry L. Price, *Understanding Ethical Failures In Leadership* (Cambridge, NY 2006), 1.

candidate claims to become the next people's representative, defender, and resources provider. However, once elected, they are nowhere to be found. After the dust settles, it becomes more difficult for the constituents to see their elected officials. Very often constituents hear statements like, *"The boss is busy. Sorry, the boss has to leave now"* and so forth. There are instances when appointments do not even mean anything. If our leaders cannot connect with their electorate after taking the office, how can they possibly defend their best interests?

Leaders ought to be men and women of character, full of moral integrity. They must work hard to keep their words and promises. If words and promises get broken, then they have the obligation to come to the people and explain why things did not go the way they hoped or expected. Unfortunately, many people go into leadership position without understanding any standards or any codes of ethics.

In the book of Exodus, God gave Moses and the children of Israel a set of rules to follow. The first four rules or commandments were related to God and the last six related to men. If six of the Ten Commandments were directly related to men, that meant God must have valued human to human relationship and protection. When E. R. Klein sees the decline of ethics in the American corporate world, he is deeply disturbed because he understands the danger that a society will face if business is conducted unethically. The collapse of ENRON, one of America's giant corporations is one example that he mentions in his book, *People First: Professional and Business Without Ethics*. Concerned with the lack of ethics in the professional and business world, Klein publishes a series of codes of conduct among which are codes for professors. After more than twenty years in the teaching field, I would like to consider myself a professional educator. That is why I chose the codes for professors from Klein's list. Klein writes:

1. *The professor*, guided by a deep conviction of the worth and dignity of the advancement of knowledge, recognizes the

special responsibility placed upon him. His primary responsibility to his subject is to seek and to state the truth as he sees it.

2. As a *teacher*, the professor encourages the free pursuit of learning in his students... He demonstrates respect for the student as an individual, and adheres to his proper role as intellectual guide and counselor... He avoids any exploitation of students for his private advantage... He protects their academic freedom.

3. As a *colleague*, the professor has obligations that drive common membership in the community of scholars. He respects and defends the free inquiry of his associates... He accepts his share of faculty responsibility for the governance of his institution.

4. As a member of his institution, the professor seeks above all to be an effective teacher and scholar.

5. As a member of his community, the professor has the rights and obligations of any citizen... As a citizen engaged in a profession that depends upon freedom for its health and integrity, the professor has a particular obligation to promote conditions of free inquiry and to further public understanding of academic freedom.[65]

If this much is required of a professor, how much more then is required of a CEO, a minister, a governor, or a head of state? Surely, responsibilities vary according to what office one holds, but all of us are required to give our very best no matter how small our responsibility appears.

Sometimes it seems difficult to take a usual approach to accomplish the difficult task. One of the churches I was part of in North Georgia started a project called "Extreme Make Over." After only one year of starting the church, Pastor Jeff Hidden thought the

---

[65] E. R. Klein, *People First: Professional and Business Ethics Without Ethics*, (University Press of America: NY, 2003), 56.

church could do more in reaching the community besides preaching. We undertook a major project. The entire church family was involved in renovating Jane's home. Because members of Victory North church were willing to partake and give themselves unto this major remodeling, Jane's home was completed in just a matter of hours. Such an experience leads me to believe that whenever there is a will, people can accomplish about anything.

When African leaders exercise a good will, Africa can then turn things upside down. From an extreme makeover of our leadership, great things will happen. And we are hopeful that African leadership can achieve this challenge in this century. Whether we belong to public, private, or non-profit sector, together, we can make an impact and leave a legacy for our future generations.

Sometimes, we may just try this leadership thing in a way we have never done before. Developing countries like Vietnam, Brazil, Mexico, or Venezuela are showing great strength in terms of leadership. Brazil, Mexico, Vietnam, and a few more have made significant economic progress while Africa spends most of its time and resources resolving regional conflicts.

In Latin America, some countries are finding their way towards a sustainable economic growth. Today, Mexico is one of the countries moving away from a still and traditional economy. In her chapter, "Flexible Production and Labor Policy: Paradoxes in the Restructuring of Mexican Industry," María Ángeles Pozas tells us that the Salinas administration aimed to increase Mexican economic efficiency. And that the government, labor, and the private sector were going to negotiate wage increases.[66]

In East Asia, Vietnam has made an impressive comeback. Good economic strategies and policies are bearing fruits. Charles Harvie and Tran Van Hoa, both Associate Professors of Economics at the University of Wollongong in Australia, mention key factors that have

---

[66] Laura Randall, *Changing Structure of Mexico: Political, Social, and Economic Prospects.* New York: (M. E. Sharpe, 1996), 137

enabled Vietnam's economy to prosper.[67] "Vietnam has moved away from a centrally planned economy with its emphasis upon collectivized agriculture, heavy industry, state control over prices, interest rates and the exchange rate, monopoly control over trade and bias against the private sector, to a market driven economy."

The general saying that success is infectious may well help Africa imitate emerging nations, which are becoming successful in many ways. Africa can benefit from the visions of emerging economies of some developing countries, and even learn from those countries, which are making a huge impact first nationally, regionally, and worldwide. Unlike the regional integrations seen in West and Central Africa, East Asia has broadened its vision to include European Union and North America Free Trade Agreement due to unpredictable exchange rates from Europe and North America. Today, many Asian products are easily found in Europe and North America. From food products to clothing, from manufactured goods to automobile industries, and from financial market to communication, Asian countries have proved to be very reliable and competitive.

Once again, without a radical and creative leadership, it will be difficult for Africa to achieve a cooperative development like what is going on in East Asia. Xiaoji Zhang explains the challenges and prospects of East Asian regional economic cooperation by two important factors: regional economic integration and economic globalization. He thinks that these two trends of development play big in world economy.[68]

In many school systems educators have developed different types of posters to encourage students to become goal achievers. One of my favorite posters lists the top ten steps to success, and I coin it the "Trying Trade" of humble people. And the poster goes in a descending order:

[67] Charles Harvie & Tran Van Hoa, *Vietnam's Reforms and Economic Growth.* New York: (MacMillan Press Ltd. 1997), 104.
[68] Xiaoji Zhang, *A Vision for Economic Cooperation in East Asia: China, Japan, and Korea:* "The Challenges and Prospects of East Asian Regional Economic Cooperation ",* (Seoul: Korea Development Institute, 2003), 21.

10. Just keep trying
9. Try to determine what is working
8. Try to determine what is not working
7. Try to find someone who has done it before
6. Try and ask for help
5. Try again tomorrow
4. Try it a little differently
3. Try once more
2. Try again
1. Try

In *The Quest for Moral Leaders: Essays on Leadership Ethics*, Joanne B. Ciulla, Terry L. Price, and Susan E. Murphy make a clear distinction between the hearts of leaders, the minds of leaders, and the bodies of leaders. In the very beginning of her introduction, Joanne Ciulla tackles the greatest strength and weakness of leaders. She simply reminds us that they were humans before they became leaders.[69] By borrowing these authors' categorizations of the leaders, our intention is not to necessarily endorse their arguments, but rather to expand and remain within our quest for a revolutionary leadership based on true morality. Unlike many revolutions, this one must radically be different in meaning, extremely rich in the form, and uniquely organized by category. Together, we must stand, and it is only together that African nations will achieve a viable and strong leadership.

---

[69] Joanne B. Ciulla, *The Quest for Moral Leaders: Essays on Leadership Ethics.* Edward Edgar Publishing Co., Northampton (2005), 1.

REFERENCES

- Adams, John D. 1986. *Transforming Leadership: From Vision to Results*, Alexander: Miles River Press, 105-106.
- African Development Bank. 1997. African Development Report, Oxford University Press, 19-28.
- Alube, Allen A. 1998. *The Murder of a National Pastor*, manuscript.
- Annunzio, Susan. 2001. *ELeadership: Proven Techniques for Creating an environment of Speed and Flexibility in the Digital Economy*, New York: The Free Press, 11-12.
- Bender, Gerald J., James S. Coleman, and Richard L. Sklar. 1985. *The African Crisis Areas and U.S. Foreign Policy* Berkley: University of California Press, 7.
- Blumenfeld, Samuel L. 1981. *Is Public Education Necessary?* Boise: The Paradigm Company, 72.
- Burt, McKinley Jr. 1989. *Black Inventors of America*, Portland: National Book company, 7.
- Carroll, Joseph. 2003. *On the Origin of Species by Means of Natural Selection, NY: Broadviewtexts, 36-37.*
- Cartwright, John. 1983. *Political Leadership in Africa*, NY: St.

Martin Press, Inc., 20.

- *Christian History & Biography*. 2003. www.ctlibrary.com/ 7847, Jan. 26, 2008.

- Ciulla, Joanne B. 2005. *The Quest for Moral Leaders: Essays on Leadership Ethics*, Northampton: Edward Edgar Publishing Co., 1. (13-45, 65-98, 113) check these pages.

- Ellsworth, Jill H. &Matthew V. Ellsworth. 1994. *The Internet Business Book*, (New York: John Wiley & Sons, Inc.), 31-32.

- Emerson, Ralph W. 2007. *www.chebucto.ns.ca/Philosophy/Sui-Generis/Emerson/Success.htm*.

- Engel, Ulf & Gorm Rye Olsen. 2004. *The African Exception*, University of Leipzig, 1.

- Engholm, Christopher & Scott Grimes. The Apprentice Hall of Directory of Online Business Information 1997, (Englewood Cliffs: Prentice Hall, 1996), 12.

- Ferkiss, Victor C. 1966. *Africa's Search for Identity*, NY: George Braziller, 14.

- Bok, Derek. 2006. BusinessWeek Online of July 10.

- Encyclopædia Britannica Online. 9 Mar. 2008. http:// www.britannica.com/eb/article

- Fick, David. 2006. *Africa: Continent of Economic Opportunity*. Johannesburg, STE Publishers, 10

- Gordon, Jacob U. 2002. African Leadership In The Twentieth Century: An Enduring Experiment In Democracy, NY: University Press of America, 155.

- Grand Rendez-Vous. 2006. "EUROPE 1-*TV5 MONDELE PARISIEN*, October 15.

- Gunther, John. 1959. *Meet The Congo and Its Neighbors*, New York: Harper & Row, 31.

- Harmick, Frank. 1999. *Proverbs: The Fountain of Life* Whitakers: Positive Action, 135.

- Harvie, Charles & Tran Van Hoa. 1997. *Vietnam's Reforms*

and Economic Growth. New York: MacMillan Press Ltd., 104.

- Heritage, Andrew. 1999. *World Atlas: Millenium Edition*, New York: DK Publishing Book, 120.
- *http://www.liberian-connection.com/tolbert/tol_speech2.htm, April 28, 2003.*
- Jening, Eugene E. 1960. *An Anatomy of Leadership: Princes, Heroes and Supermen*, NY: McGraw-Hillbook, 221.
- Kanyogonya, Elizabeth. *What's Africa's Problem?* 2000. University of Minnesota Press, 10.
- Kets de Vries, Manfred F. R. 2006. *The Leader on the Couch*, West Sussex: Jossey-Bass, 52.
- Klein, E. R. 2003. *People First: Professional and Business Ethics Without Ethics*, NY: University Press of America, 56.
- Leeper Ward Robert & Madison Peter. 1959. *Toward Understanding Human Personalities*. New York: Applet onCentury-Crofts, Inc.
- *LitScape*, A publication of ProLiteracy America, Summer 2003.
- Machel, Graca. 2001. *The Impact of War on Children*. New York: Palgrave, 182.
- Marina, Ottaway. 1999. *Africa's New Leaders: Democracy or State Reconstruction? Carnagie Endowment*, Washington, 29-44.
- Maxwell, John C. 1993. *Developing The Leader Within You*, Nashville: Thomas Nelson Publishers, 1.
- Maxwell, John C. *Today Matters: 12 Daily Practices To Guarantee Tomorrow's Success*, 4-6. See Videos
- Mazrui, Ali A. 1980. *The African Condition*, New York: Cambridge University Press, 46-47.
- McNally, Rand. Character, Sketches from the Pages of Scripture (Rand McNally & Co. 1978), TC
- N'Diaye, Boubacar, Abdoulaye Saine, Mathurin Houngnikpo. 2005. *"Not Yet Democracy": West Africa Slow*

Farwell to Authoritarianism, Carolina Academic Press, Durham, 156.

- Norton, Ginger. 2004. coreknowledge.org/ck/resrcs/lessons/ 04_4_EarlyMedieval.pdf
- Olasky, Marvin. 2003. *Carver's Affirmations*, World, 36.
- Olsen, Ted. *Christian History*, Issue 79, Vol. XXII, # 3, 14.
- Padover, Saul K. 1963. *The Meaning of Democracy: An Appraisal of American Experience*, NY: Frederick A. Praeger Publishers, 45.
- Padover, Saul K. 1964. *The Meaning of Democracy: An Appraisal of the American Experience*, New York: Frederick A. Paerger, Publishers, 98.
- Polgreen, lidya. 2006. *International Herald Tribune Nov. 23.*
- Price, Terry L. 2006. *Understanding Ethical Failures In Leadership*, NY: Cambridge, 1.
- *ProLiteracy Publication Worldwide*, Summer 2003, 1.
- Randall, Laura. 1996. *Changing Structure of Mexico: Political, Social, and Economic Prospects*. New York: M. E. Sharpe, 137
- Ravage, John W. 1997. *Black Pioneers: Images of the Black Experience on the North American Frontier*, Salt Lake City: The University of Utah Press, 73.
- Segal, Ronald. 1995. The Black Diaspora, New York: Farrar, Straus and Giroux.
- Sinclair, Amanda. 2005. *Doing Leadership Differently: Gender, Power and Sexuality in a Changing Business Culture*, Melbourne University Press, 113-114.
- Tichy, Noel M. 1997. *The Leadership Engine: How Winning Companies Build Leaders at Every Level*, New York: Harper Business, 3.
- United Nations, Demographic Yearbook 2004, New York 2007, 5

- US Census Bureau, The United States in the International Context, Feb. 2002
- UN Statistics Division, Depart of Economic & Social Affairs, 20 June 2007.
- Wangome, Jimmi. 2006. *Military Coups In Africa— The African "Neo-Colonialism" That Is Self-Inflicted*, Kenya Army, CSC 1985. See internet, Dec.16, 2006.
- Watson, Charles E. 1991. *Managing With Integrity: Insights from America's CEOs*, NY: Praeger, 3.
- Wheatley, Margaret J. 2006. *Leadership and the New Science (Discovering Order in a Chaotic World)*, San Francisco: Berrett-Koelher Publishers, Inc., 139. www.homestead.com/wysinger/berlin-conference-doc.html

www.ingramcontent.com/pod-product-compliance
Lightning Source LLC
LaVergne TN
LVHW021745160125
801442LV00001B/120

* 9 7 9 8 8 8 9 2 5 2 1 2 2 *